Best always-
Bill Cooper
Chief of Police (ret)

Leading Beyond Tradition

Exceeding Expectations in Any Economy

William E. Cooper

Chief of Police (ret)

Leading Beyond Tradition

Exceeding Expectations in Any Economy

William E. Cooper

Published by 3-Star Publications
PO Box 1001, Mukilteo, WA 98275
www.leadingbeyondtradition.com

Ordering Information
To order additional copies,
www.leadingbeyondtradition.com

ISBN: 978-0-9847668-3-3
LCCN/PCN: 2011945311

Leading Beyond Tradition

Exceeding Expectations in Any Economy

More praise for Leading Beyond Tradition

*B*ill Cooper's management model is adaptable to both the public and private sectors. Combining the best elements of LEAN Six Sigma, Business Intelligence Decision Support, Community or Employee Involvement, and Predictive Analytics in one model is a tremendous and effective tool. It provides its practitioners with increased efficiency and productivity while substantially reducing operating costs. Executives and Managers should look toward this model. Michael Kline, Former United States Marshal

"Bill's convergence of Lean Six Sigma, CompStat and Community Oriented Policing is designed to revolutionize the effectiveness and efficiency of law enforcement. The Cooper Model is impressive on two fronts: 1) the ease of its implementation, and 2) the immediate return on capital invested. Law enforcement leadership across the country would do well to invest in the concepts offered up by Bill and his program. I was amazed at how Bill was able to simplify the complex ideas of Lean Six Sigma and overlay them with our existing CompStat model to where all the command staff and line supervisors could not only easily understand it but to start to immediately utilize the lessons learned. During his two-day seminar

Exceeding Expectations in Any Economy

we identified waste in our existing processes and implemented workflow improvements that should save over $200,000.00! You cannot afford to not implement this in your organization."
Chief Jeff Baker, Morrow, GA Police Department

"Mr. Cooper's book takes into account all of the customers and the internal staff to bring to the forefront salient issues that affect us all. His insight on how to implement strategies such as Lean Six Sigma into the traditional organizational structure of policing is insightful and his ideas bring about results. He delves into process mapping, problem solving, and handling the limits of budget and resources. His study of the 911 system and the impact of its use for emergency and more often non-emergency calls bring home the fact that Policing is bursting at the seams with calls that are non-relevant." Bette Daoust, PhD

"In LEADING BEYOND TRADITION, retired Chief of Police William Cooper has written a call to action- one that should be read by law enforcement officials everywhere. With his skilful integration of Lean Six Sigma, CompStat, and Community Involvement, Cooper offers a radical new vision for modernizing police work for the 21st century. Striking a good balance between theory and applied science, LEADING BEYOND TRADITION

Leading Beyond Tradition

Exceeding Expectations in Any Economy

includes several case studies that clearly illustrate Cooper's timely message. The wisdom found in LEADING BEYOND TRADITION applies to a wide range of civil servants, including police, firefighters, and EMS, and should be required reading as well for government officials, military personnel, disaster response teams and any leader involved in visioning new ways of keeping America safe." Tim Warneka, author

"Cooper has provided a book on a complex subject that removes much of the mystery and perceived complexity that roadblocks our ability to achieve positive improvements in our organizations. This book should be considered required reading for first level supervisors and up through to the executive level in any organization that provides a service to others."

"Cooper's book represents what has long been missing in the fields of public and private service, the specific tools and processes necessary to achieve success in an organization that is tasked with providing a service to others. Unlike so many books written by so called `experts' that reflect upon their individual paths to success that don't always relate to the challenges we are facing, this book is applicable to anyone who desires to

achieve and succeed within any service related organization." Rob DeGroot, Fife, WA

"The Cooper Model is the solution right now. It has the versatility of being top down or bottom up. It is not the standard adaptation of police management models. It is its own powerful management model. It should be standard orientation. This model develops how to look at management of your organization with budgeting and staffing in line with the current environment. Cooper is consistent and achieves more with the resources he already has. He will show you how to better target your resources, and dramatically reduce crime and cost, without any increase in staff."Bob Mahoney (Ret) F. B. I., General Manager, Port Authority NY/NJ

"Administrators who follow this model will subsequently be able to transform their departments into more effective, efficient, and proactive agencies that are more in line with their missions, and are driven by the results of their actions".

"Chief Cooper presents a very through and impressive leadership and management model that appears to be beneficial to all police

departments and other organizations". Annette
Frisbie, graduate thesis

*"Initially introduced as a management model for
law enforcement, the model is highly adaptable
and invaluable to other government entities and
organizations".*

*"The Leading Beyond Tradition management
model is a system of business processes
and tools that can be applied to every aspect,
function, and task of the organization".*

Table of Contents

This book is dedicated to many fine people. The list starts with my lifelong companion and best friend, my beautiful wife Patty. Both my daughters, Kelly and Kristi, and their fine husbands Nick and Pete, who have contributed so much to my life and happiness. To my mom and dad, who sacrificed so much for us and taught us values, principles, and the courage to do what's right all the time.

To all the people of the United States who give so much and ask so little in return, you have earned the right, the right to the best leadership and management our country can provide.

To my friends and colleagues in the public and corporate world, I am proud of you and your accomplishments. I need to especially call those whose contributions cannot be measured in an ordinary sense.

Fatuesi Fatuesi - you are an extremely fine and honorable leader to whom I owe a great deal. Your inspiration and remarkable ethics are the model everyone should follow. It is because of you that this model flourished in the private sector. You and your second in command, Cindy Olson, motivated the officers to produce extremely fine results. John Wilhite, whose tireless devotion to doing what's right and his support of his people and company should be the standard we all need to follow. Claire Walter, who helped create the predictive models, gave life to significant parts of this book. The people all work for Guardsmark, LLC., and they are the best.

To my teams in the private sector, calling out Bob Pemberton, Bob Afflerbach, Brian Hall, and Tom Rowe, you are truly great people and I consider it an honor to have worked with you.

To all the law enforcement officers and managers, you are among the best this country has to offer and I am proud of each of you. The officers of my police department went through considerable change and did it with high standards and success. They did the job with pride and took ownership and I will never forget them. Those officers I was fortunate to teach over the years taught me as much or more than I taught them. The students in my graduate school classes did the same. I am grateful for the lessons.

I also want to acknowledge NYPD Commissioner and Los Angeles Police Chief Bill Bratton, who is responsible for the creation of CompStat, which served as the inspiration for The Cooper Model's Business Intelligence Decision Support System. I was fortunate to spend time with Chief Bratton and am grateful to him; he is a true leader.

One man who has been a mentor, an advisor, and more importantly, my friend, is Bob Mahoney. He served as a career FBI agent and General Manager of the Port Authority NY/NJ, and is a survivor of the 9/11 attacks. Bob is a successful writer in his own right and has offered input to my writing and this management model on many occasions. I am indebted to him.

There are likely many to whom I have not properly acknowledged and will simply say that you have been an inspiration to me and I thank you.

This book is dedicated to teaching and showing you what works. For you – dedicate anything you touch the best it can possibly be. Apply exacting standards consistently at all times at all levels. No one can ask for more.

THINK
clearly about
YOUR
purpose or mission,
YOUR
strategy & your stakeholders,
and **what** their
REQUIREMENTS
might be.

Bill Cooper is a retired Chief of Police, who also brings senior management experience from the private sector. Bill is recognized for leadership and high performing organizations, and is the author of the award winning book, Leading Beyond Tradition. Bill is a management expert who has consulted with and taught organizations on how to optimize performance with resources and staff an organization already has, especially in difficult economic times. He created the Cooper Management Model and has been featured on radio and television, and the Cooper Model has been the subject of several graduate school theses.

The depth and breadth of Chief Cooper's background has been described as being in the top 5% of the most diverse and comprehensive qualifications relevant to management. With his model he turned around the police department, and did the same in two Fortune 200 companies. He has had a significant impact on organizations he has taught and consulted with.

Bill holds an MBA and a second Master's Degree in Public Administration, and is a graduate of the FBI National Academy and Washington State Law Enforcement Executive Command College. He is trained in both

Exceeding Expectations in Any Economy

Lean Six Sigma and is a Six Sigma Black Belt, both of which are used in Fortune 500 corporations. In addition, he has been an adjunct professor, teaching Masters level courses in Organizational Development, High Performance Organizations, and Executive Leadership. He has lectured extensively on management topics and how to make organizations efficient and effective.

Bill provides keynote addresses, lectures, training and consulting services. His website is **www.leadingbeyondtradition.com.**

Rob McKenna, WA State Attorney General

When I became the Attorney General for the State of Washington, our office, as well as the other departments in state government, were underperforming. Government operated with the traditional "we've always done it that way" philosophy, and there was little to no experience in management being learned from the private sector. The private sector lives in the competitive world where revenues are earned and not provided by taxes. Taxpayer dollars in government are being wasted and productivity is too low.

I brought to the Attorney General's Office a system of continuous quality improvement. We've also adopted a Lean methodology for working that focuses on being cost conscious and accountable to our constituents. Most importantly, we've brought the spirit of innovation to the office. As a result of these changes and by empowering employees, we've become the best public law office in America. Our Attorney General's Office is committed to continuous improvement, a relentless search for cost savings and efficiencies, performance management and accountability. Productivity has increased markedly, costs are down significantly, service quality is up, and employee morale is higher.

I met Bill Cooper, who is a former Chief of Police and Senior Manager in the private sector. Bill applied Lean

Six Sigma to his organizations with excellent results. He believed that the application of proven business principles to government organizations would work, and proved it with award-winning success. Bill also believed that a graphics-rich Business Intelligence Decision Support System would focus existing resources, and proved that Lean Six Sigma would free time and money to help accomplish his organization's mission.

Bill looked honestly at how his organizations were performing and added Community or Employee Involvement to his management model. He found that a large percent of his staff and resources were consumed by activities better handled by volunteers or the private sector. By creating real, long-term partnerships with the community and private sector employees, he was able to reduce the volume of activity his department was handling by large margins. Doing so further reduced the burden on resources and saved considerable time and cost. Finally, Bill added a highly impressive predictive analytics element that would statistically forecast where the probability of a law enforcement event or incident would occur.

Each of these proven principles works well in any organization or as a stand-alone system. By combining them into one management model, Bill has created the ability for any organization to succeed in any economy. Your organization, regardless of size, will see dramatic results in terms of faster service, better quality, and lower costs.

I highly recommend that managers in both the public and private sectors read this book. I hope you will enjoy the same results we have achieved in the Attorney General's Office.

The **SUM TOTAL** of our **EFFORTS** has not **produced** the **OUTCOMES** we **need. So** it's time to **DO THINGS** d i f f e r e n t l y .

"Action requires creativity and logical thinking." Unknown

I had the privilege of serving in law enforcement for nearly 30 years, including time as Chief of Police. Part of that privilege was serving with some of the finest, most incredible people you'll find in America.

I've met world class police officers and administrators, staff and corporate employees, all dedicated to serving their communities and customers to the best of their abilities. As the chief and corporate senior manager, I lived through the economic ups and downs, and struggled financially the same as many organizations are doing today. They face the challenges of continuing to provide high levels of service with ever growing demands, incidents and activities and often reduced budgets.

I succeeded in these times by deciding to look at management differently, by not following a traditional model, and by making adjustments to changing conditions. Much of what organizations face is predictable and by looking forward and proactively, the difference is substantial.

It is because of these struggles and the good people I was fortunate enough to work with or teach that this work became possible. I believe that our collective intellect, skills, and abilities and education – our diversity – working together there is no problem we cannot solve.

Exceeding Expectations in Any Economy

In learning that the more traditional models of management are often less than efficient and not very effective in many cases, I looked how I was managing a public or private organization and concluded we could do better – much better. The organization was not solving problems; we were reacting to them after the fact. In many instances we didn't look at the real problem. We were not focused on the level of sophistication of our employees, nor were we effectively using technology. We were not truly identifying what the root problems were, but were reacting to symptoms of larger or deeper issues. We really didn't know what the root causes were and yet at budget time every year were asking taxpayers or administrators to give us ever more of their money to continue to produce the same results.

Given the events executives and managers are facing in the 21st century, we are faced with the need for adjusting both philosophically and operationally. New and challenging economic concerns, the ability to keep good employees, and ever-growing competition for services continue to test us. Economic reality is forcing organizations to do something new and different.

With this in mind, I began to look at creating a management model that optimizes resources and staff, provides higher quality and quantity of service at lower cost, and transforms a reactive model into an intelligence-based proactive deployment model that produces substantial results in achieving the organizational mission.When I launched this model I was going on a journey that I didn't know where it would take me, but having been there, I'll give you what I learned.

The Cooper Management Model sought to take proven business principles and apply them originally into the public sector. The first of three elements was the use of the widely successful CompStat system, developed by the New York City Police Department, designed to focus staff and resources when and where they were needed and produce measureable results. NYPD was able to reduce crime in the city by more than 50%. I used it in my department with some success, but recognized the limitation that in many cases we were simply displacing the issue to another location. We could not sustain that type of operation and were not identifying what the real problems were, much less addressing them.

> "Leading Beyond Tradition is a continuous improvement and refinement process designed specifically to dramatically improve the organization's efficiency, free up money in the existing budget, and invite and benefit from employee and community involvement and support". Lt. Peter Fischer, Bremerton, WA Police Department

I looked for a root causation system and found the Six Sigma methodology, created by Motorola in the 1980s, and now widely used in Fortune 500 corporations with considerable success. I read a number of books about Six Sigma, and ultimately trained through Motorola

University to achieve their Black Belt level. While it is mathematically oriented, I was able to simplify the methodology and extract much of the more complex math, and still successfully apply the systems and tools. I applied the methodology to CompStat with success and began to apply it to the internal business processes with the department. The results, some immediate, were astonishing, and began to anchor a belief that the direction we were going would actually work, that we could do the job without continually asking the taxpayers for more money every year to produce the same low outcomes.

The third element of the Cooper Model was to look at the widely used Community Oriented Policing system that had been in law enforcement for more than 25 years. Virtually all departments use COP in some fashion, but the intent of COP – partnering with the communities, did not seem to be working. As this book will demonstrate why it didn't work, I created the Community Involvement piece that did. Dramatic cost avoidance and savings, as well as time freed for staff proved to be one of the larger successes.

When I was recruited into the private sector and retired from the police department, I took the model with me and made minor modifications for the business world, and realized the same levels of success in delivering better and more service at lower cost. Since its inception I have continued to develop and evolve the model, which now includes the use of predictive analytics and a far more effective Business Intelligence Decision Support System to replace CompStat, and now use predictive analytics in some circumstances.

Each element of the model in and of itself is powerful. The true strength of the model lies in its convergence of the various parts into one approach. In the case studies and examples in this book, the reader will discover a wide array of benefits.

The Cooper Model and its components are described in the chapters of this book, and the reader is provided examples and case studies showing how effective it really is, that through its application, and public or private sector organization has the ability to provide substantially better service at a lower cost. The book also discusses the peripheral and significant other benefits.

The reader will find that the model provides the opportunity to achieve considerable benefits if leaders actually apply it. It does oblige leaders to make minor adjustments in their thinking and the ability to overcome change, a shift away from the status quo.

The book is not intended as a criticism of current management practices – it intends to provide a different approach, using proven business principles combined into a model that maximizes each, and as a whole. By applying these into one management system, the resulting outcomes are substantially enhanced.

The one element common to organizations, in good times or bad, is the recognition that change is necessary – something needs to be done differently. Change is often problematic. People want it – until it affects them personally. We get comfortable doing what we've been doing for a long time and changing can be disruptive and may be viewed in several different ways – few of them good. Change requires a movement away from the status quo.

Organizational development research tells us that the majority of efforts to change fail to achieve their objective. The single largest failure point is a lack of communication of a new and powerful business management model – one that provides a level of predictable outcomes. Communication is always what is received – not necessarily what was sent; a critical understanding. Telling staff or the community what to expect and how it will impact them, then letting them help build it provides all a chance to develop success. "Companies do not become world leaders and renowned for their performance without a great deal of expenditure of effort from their staff."[1]

---

[1] Atkinson, Phillip, Managing Resistance to Change, Management Services Spring 2005

More importantly getting people to change their business practices to help build it enhances the chances for success exponentially. In my experience having done so across public and private sector organizations, the model works well. Employees or community members want to be part of something special and this opens the door for them to build outcomes with pride and ownership contributing to organizational success.

For example, in one of the Fortune 200 organizations I managed corporate security and the contract security officers. Security is viewed as a cost center and contributes little to nothing to the bottom financial line in the eyes of many. Security officers patrolled, they check access badges, and responded to the typically security calls involving employees being locked out of their offices, or needed a delivery somewhere. In this company they were counting unused parking spaces, pinning flyers for various business unit events on the walls, and turning clocks back or forward at daylight savings time. They were comfortable in the role, but attrition was noteworthy and their performance minimal. They were good employees and were performing to expectations of the company.

When I was hired and brought the Cooper Model to Security, I began to refocus resources. I wrote new Mission and Vision Statements, developed new Goals and Objectives, and began to transform a risk-averse, totally reactive model of security to a proactive, problem identification, problem solution, results based operation. Everything was premised on the use of analyzed business intelligence. I involved the contract security team in the development of these documents and new philosophies and received excellent feedback and input. It was as if – again – employees were asking to be heard and became identifiable stakeholders.

We developed performance metrics based on true security and safety issues and concerns and held the officers accountable for proactively finding them, escalating them to the right people, then following up to assure correction. We measured and viewed this performance in our new Business Intelligence Decision Support System. The older employees who did not wish to participate were moved to other organizations and new officers were brought in who fit the philosophies and systems. We essentially got the right people in, the wrong people out, and the right people in the right places.

Over time, real security and safety issues were identified and reduced and stayed at lowered levels for succeeding years. The ability to breach the company was dropped by 95%. If one did breach a building, the ability to remove assets was reduced by 98% - pure cause and effect.

The same is possible – and proven – in my law enforcement experiences and is possible in local government departments or the government itself, as well in any business unit of the private sector. Applying the Cooper Model succeeds every time it has been used.

Organizations fail in many ways because of trying to stay with what worked in the past, and hasn't been working. If organizations used such methodologies or practices as Lean Six Sigma or a true business intelligence system or worked differently within their communities or employees, they would not be in poor positions, reducing their workforces, reducing service levels, or losing profit or resourcing. Times are changing and they will never be the same again. Don't stay the course; change the course; change your rules and embrace a new strategy. Play the game while there's still time on the clock. Failure to change leads your organization to deteriorate – don't get yourself in a position of continually explaining failure. This book is a call to action and can help solve your financial and resource problems as revenues shrink and resources are being lost. There are opportunities for any organization to improve itself with faster service, higher quality, all at a lower cost. Think about it; this is the time for critical thinking. Stop being too busy keeping the organization the way it is in these times, and start making it what it's entirely capable of being.

Chapter 1:

The Cooper Management Model

"Leadership is the capacity to translate vision into reality." Warren G. Bennis

I - Overview:

Global companies and law enforcement agencies use theCooper Model for strategic planning and actionable performance measurement. The Cooper Model designs specific programs based on real-time data collection models, and provides training and consultation on the identification, reduction, or elimination of costly business process systems. In addition, this successful model optimizes performance of existing resources, providing an organization a higher standard of performance, enhanced financial management, and significant outcomes.

The model is further enhanced through the use of predictive analytics in certain circumstances and the involvement of either employees in a company or members of a community. By partnering with people, the organization has the ability to place much of their activity with people who are better positioned to handle it. This, in turn, allows an organization to focus its finite resources and staff where they're needed.

How the Cooper Model works

II - Business Intelligence Decision Support System:

The Business Intelligence Decision Support System:

- improves employee and/or community involvement in their own protection and safety;
- analyzes performance metrics; and
- provides predictive analytics and spatial mapping.

This model provides:

- success of programs with hard numbers;
- documented improvement in effectiveness;
- measurable risk and vulnerability reduction;

Exceeding Expectations in Any Economy

- effective allocation of resources; and
- identified, documented cost reductions and return on investment (ROI).

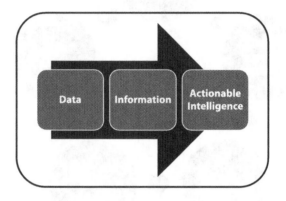

The Business Intelligence Decision Support System fully justifies an organization's spend by contributing to the bottom line.

III – Actionable Performance Measurement:

What is the Business Intelligence Decision Support System?

- An analytical system, customized to meet unique requirements to better define priorities and quantify threats and vulnerabilities.
- An integrated intelligence base, applying statistical information about your business to form this unique and successful management model.

- An identification of mitigation strategies and action planning to support prevention and eliminate vulnerability.
- A tool to capture and verify comparative analysis.
- Application of your previous statistical data, evaluating this data against the business Strategic Plan.

This system employs verification techniques in existing practices. These components enable you to identify cost reduction, improve effectiveness and provide data necessary for initiating changes in cultural behavior.

By collecting defined metrics and conducting a simple analysis, trends and/or patterns are easily identified. This allows for the focused deployment of resources and staff to identifiable, identified problems. It shows clear gaps, allowing questions to be asked about performance – what changed and why? What needs to be done to close the gap and how will it be sustained? What is important to remember is the integrity of the data being analyzed. Using accurate data and information drives actionable intelligence, allowing for faster and better decisions.

IV – Lean Six Sigma:

The Cooper Model identifies and improves an organization's inefficient and resource consuming programs and procedures through the widely used

Lean Six Sigma tools and process mapping protocols. Unnecessary components are highlighted for removal or revision, resulting in time and cost improvement.

V – Predictive and Comparative Analytics:

The Cooper Model includes templates to enhance problem identification and provide predictive and comparative analytics using defined metrics. The metrics are verified for accuracy and tracked over time. Causes are defined and addressed by using the near real-time data. The program measures the impact of increased and focused activity.

At regularly scheduled meetings, leadership reviews the data, refines tactics, strategies and processes, with the focus on getting results. These meetings verify the metrics and potential collection problems. Results or action proposed to address vulnerabilities are analyzed for impact.

The Cooper Model is motivating for supervisory personnel because it's based on active participation of all personnel. Few people in an organization know the issues and vulnerabilities better than the line staff. As they have insight into logical remedial actions at the source, the feedback is valuable and highly motivating.

For example, they may suggest solutions to ongoing problems, which deliver measurable reductions of that particular problem. These solutions all result in reduction of cost and time employees may better spend on the product or service. It is a truism that those who are closest to the problem are in the best position to offer solutions. It is also true that these issues and inefficiencies all come with a cost, and by reducing or eliminating that cost, an organization's profit margin or budget are stabilized and predictable.

The statistical analysis of pre-defined metrics describing the type, level and impact of, for example, crime, workplace violence, or other ongoing problem within an organization or community will predict future events. Based on historic trends, the model calculates statistical probability of a future event occurring. This results in easily actionable change.

VI - GETTING STARTED:

The Cooper Modelbegins with an assessment and the development of a strategic plan based on the organization's identified objectives.

One of the key points of analysis is information collection including specific metrics based on specificissues. Conduct an on-site review of current incident data and collection practices, incident reporting and processes used in your organization's duties.

Exceeding Expectations in Any Economy

The product of this assessment and gap analysis is a report that serves as the basis of a strategic plan, including data collection processes to be used for performance measurement.

VII - BUILDING A STRATEGIC PLAN AND ACTIONABLE PERFORMANCE MEASUREMENTS:

The organization's self-assessment results will:

- assist management prioritizing;
- focus resources;
- establish performance review tools;
- improve processes; and
- monitor progress.

The Cooper Model and its Business Intelligence Decision Support System:

- collects data from many information sources;
- monitors progress against established goals;
- provides regular reports; and most importantly
- alerts management to deviations and statistical probability of security breaches.

Provide training to ensure the accuracy and reliability of data collection and reporting is captured. This process empowers the rank and file personnel as the prime identifiers of routine issues, and their proposed resolution. This active involvement engenders enthusiastic participation by personnel and helps ensure the accuracy of data collection, critical to your success.

VIII - OPERATIONS AND CONTINUOUS IMPROVEMENT:

The Cooper Model provides the vital tools in operations, performance optimization and cost reduction.

This is nota static document written by committee and filed away in a cabinet. Using the Cooper Model provides an organization the ability to :

- guide resource deployment;
- helps continuously improve processes and focus;
- saves on critical budgets and costs;
- save on the time to complete work;
- provide organization members the ability to help identify problems and provide solutions.

Over the last 3 years, 3 large corporations and law enforcement agencies using the Business Intelligence Decision Support System each saved an average of **$350,000** annually using the Cooper Model program.

SUMMARY: The Cooper Model program will deliver the critical process and tools for a successful strategic plan with actionable performance measurements. The program will help you:

- develop and continuously refine a comprehensive strategic plan;
- focus and optimize resources;
- track performance, including trends and deviations;
- predict events and incidents with statistical probability; and
- reduce time and cost.

The Cooper Model designs decisions, industry standards and a reliable, predictable management model – new best practices. It allows managers and executives to act with confidence and credibility.

Place
RESPONSIBILITY
for your
FUTURE SQUARELY
in your
OWN SHOULDERS.

Chapter 2:

What's the Problem?

"The world hates change, yet it is the only thing that has brought progress." Charles F. Kettering

For both the public and private sectors the problem is essentially the same, but from two distinctly different points of view – revenue, money, the economic forecast. The public sector organizations are essentially guaranteed a budget where private sector organizations are not. Public sector provides service without a profit, where the private sector provides service for a profit. The private sector is frequently seeking more efficiency – lower cost – while it is not a priority in the public sector. Both are trying to meet growing needs with diminishing resources. Both have cultures that are resistant to creativity and both need change.

In both cases problems and concerns are known. In most cases traditional management models are followed with the expectation outcomes should or will improve – but ultimately have not resulted in improvements. This is largely attributable to the frequent adjustments of organizations in attempts to meet immediate needs, rather than look at the larger picture. As fiscal pressures grow, leaders are demanding that we have a way to indicate how effective we are performing.

What is the effect today and what will it be going forward? How do we plan? How do we budget? Where will the money come from? How will it be spent? And, most importantly, how does it affect you from a consumer or taxpayer perspective?

How do we as executives and managers answer these questions? What are our decisions going to be? How will we survive, much less flourish? Most importantly, what is learned when people and resources have been lost? Leaders think to themselves that this isn't the way things are supposed to be; this isn't supposed to happen.

Organizations, both public and private need to be asking the following questions on a frequent basis to determine what the honest answers are.

- Is what you're doing working – to the extent you expect or want?
- Is your organization achieving its goals?
- What are the results – really?
- Is the organization operating as efficiently and effectively as it is capable of doing?
- What amount of work has waste, re-work, or redundancy in it?
- How will it be reduced?
- What is it costing the organization?
- Is the organization reactive or proactive?
- How will it be made proactive?

- The organization's service costs money to produce and deliver. How much should it cost?
- Has the organization optimized the resources it already has?

A city council in Washington State voted to cut its police department from the budget and contract with the Sheriff's Office – a move that they believed would save the city about $375,000 annually – this city, like many others, is in financial trouble due to economy-based lower revenues. But is this the only cost such a move comes with? A thorough analysis of the department shows that there is more than that in savings if the department applied this model, and the citizens of the city, most of whom did not want to lose their department, are satisfied customers.

Other cities:

- "Budget cuts are forcing police around the U.S. to stop responding to fraud, burglary and theft call and focus on violent crime".[2]
- "What happens to Camden after police cuts? Camden, N.J.'s decision to lay off 168 police officers during a budget crisis may be the most drastic example of police cutbacks in recent times".[3]

---

2 USA Today 8-25-2010
3 www.msnbc.com 1-20-2011

- "Putting the brakes on speeding tickets. Police cutbacks blamed for huge drop in citations."[4]
- "Oakland Police: Don't Call, Report Crimes Online. Oakland police chief is making some dire claims about what his force will and will not respond to if layoffs go as planned".[5]
- "Lynnwood Police facing devastating budget cuts that would decimate the department".[6]

These are just a few of the examples of how local governments and their police departments across the country are reacting to the news of budget reductions due to the economy. Look at the nature of the response in each case – it is to cut critical police services. There is little effort going in to looking at the total picture, and what other opportunities are possible to the organization.

In examining the record for the private sector, the problem is similar.

- "Layoffs spread to more sectors of the economy. Furloughs, wage reductions, hiring freezes and shorter working hours simply did not do enough. With orders for new products and services drying up and financing tight, employers are looking to shrink their costs drastically and are slashing their payrolls..."[7]

4   www.articles.boston,com 7-31-2011
5   www.newsone.com 7-13-2010
6   www.lynnwoodtoday.com 7-26-2010
7   Rampell, Catherine, New York Times, page A1, 1-27-2009

Exceeding Expectations in Any Economy

In reality, it isn't just an economic concern. As long as the economy was good and the money available, operating an organization was good and fairly simple to do. It's when the fiscal resources began to diminish that problems grew.

The problem is that leaders continue to manage with the same philosophies and strategies they always have, and results continue to deteriorate as costs go up. It is important for leaders to take a hard and thorough look at the reality of their individual situations and adjust accordingly. Hard times are a challenge where learning and growth need to happen. Progress is the natural order of a growing, healthy business.[8]

Research in organizational development suggests that 90% of culture change initiatives fail in achieving their objectives. This is largely due to several factors, including lack of communication with those affected by the change, lack of getting staff involved in planning and executing change, and executives and/or managers not committing to the change longer term. The beliefs of many leaders are limiting.

As stated, the economy is not the stand alone problem. Given that it is the current reality, the failure to make adjustments to accommodate that reality is a significant

---

8   Siebold, Steve, 177 Mental Toughness Secrets of the World Class. P.124. London Free Press, 2005

problem as well. To make the proper changes executives and managers need to identify exactly what that looks like. The organization labors under these economic issues, and they appear to be impeding the ability to move forward. If money is considered the main concern, then money stifles growth and change. Leaders are tested bydifficulty.

What are your organizational priorities and business concerns – the highest priority problems that must be addressed if success is to be achieved? It comes down to leadership – the ability to stop doing what isn't working and trying something new. When executives and managers confront the reality of their organization through an honest assessment, the right decisions become evident. Stop doing what isn't working and start doing what is proven to work.

Start by looking at the United States economy and the path it has been and is on. Ask whether it will improve in the foreseeable future or not. Economists and the U.S. Office of Budget and Management state that with the current trend of spending exceeding revenue the economy will not improve consistently or significantly. In addition, other effects of the economy include reductions in staff, lowered performance, lower morale, reduced profits for the private sector and lower budgets for the public sector.

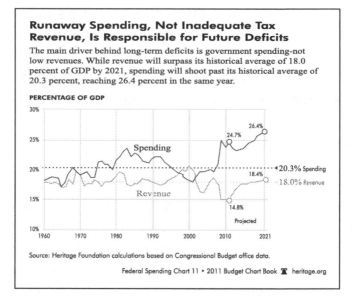

Graphic courtesy of the Heritage Foundation

With this future in mind, the Cooper Model provides the executives and managers an ongoing improvement model that changes the status quo by finding new ways of looking at old problems. The model gives executives and managers the tools to find what the real problems are, eliminating suboptimal activities that provide little or no value to the organization. The Cooper Management Model provides the organization with an unswerving focus on its return on investment it makes to succeed. There are no more excuses about why things can't be done, so the focus shifts to how it is done. The responsibility for the success of the organization sits squarely on the shoulders of the executives, managers, and staff members.

The bottom line becomes the bottom line. By following this management system, costs are reduced or avoided altogether, significant time is freed up to redeploy your existing resources to your essential needs, you clearly demonstrate to your customers and constituents enhanced levels of credibility and performance, employee morale improves and attrition lowers. Your organization maximizes its resources to optimize its outcomes and everyone wins.

The Cooper Management Model is an agile response to a changing financial environment. It allows you to transform your organization to outperform the competition in the private sector and outperform historic outcomes in the public sector. As an executive or local elected official you will tell your customers or constituents that your organization was able to succeed where others don't. You are being judged on results and the expectation is growing. The absence of results really renders leadership meaningless. There is a difference between an organization that reinvents the way it thinks and operates and the one that maintains the status quo.

In short, given the growing burden placed on organizations to produce, in a poor economy, and continuing to apply traditional management models organizations are literally incapable of being the best.

Are there better ways to manage, to deliver superior service and performance? Is there a better way to maximize the financial resources an organization is given? Can an organization restore its belief in its purpose and mission, then deliver on it? The unequivocal answer to all these questions is an unqualified yes.

This book provides those answers. The real benefit of the Cooper Management Model is its unique application by combining the successful business principles widely used in both the public and private sectors. It is that combination that capitalizes on each element to give users the advantage others don't have.

We MUST **identify,** **reduce,** or **eliminate** all suboptimal **processes** or **services;** REMOVE **unnecessary** activities that **provide** **no value** to the organization.

Chapter 3:

Lean Six Sigma

"For organizations to reach their potential, learning and ideas must preside over the status quo and tradition." Jack Welch

The need for more efficient and effective systems and processes continues to grow in virtually all organizations. The need for delivering the highest quality service at the lowest cost also continues to grow. Eliminating what does not add value. What is wasteful or redundant is becoming the priority for executives and managers. Lean Six Sigma creates tremendous positive change, an enormous jump in capabilities and dramatic reduction in costs. It is a system that is proven to work.

Both the public and private sectors find themselves under increasing demand to reduce cost and increase service. Historically, the public sector has reacted by eliminating services rather than look at the way business is done. Many in the private sector do the same, but are making significant adjustments to accommodate the need to exist, much less flourish. Organizations do not understand that they are a series of processes that work together to deliver services that are efficient, effective, and properly use the dollars they are allocated. It is a systematic approach to de-bottleneck the organization's processes and systems.

Given its rich history, Lean Six Sigma now reaches what appears to be the most successful methodology in business and government history. More than 50% of the Fortune 500 companies use Lean Six Sigma to drive improvement, and more and more local governments are reaching out to adopt the methodology. "Lean Six Sigma forces organizations to examine cost, quality, and constituent service collectively and continuously. Cost equal efficiency. Quality equals effectiveness. Constituent service equals service."[9]

What is it and why use it?

Six Sigma originated as an improvement methodology at Motorola in the mid-1980s and was designed to statistically analyze data to identify and eliminate defects, and reduce variation, all through the identification of real root causes. In short, Six Sigma equals precision in your work. By eliminating or reducing variation, dramatic improvements are made that allow a decrease in the chance of introducing errors in the future. It makes the system predictable. It allows for the development of a philosophy of getting it right the first time.

Lean Six Sigma is used to identify waste and non-value add steps in processes, increases the speed to completion, reducing both time and cost in the eyes of the consumer. Lean Six Sigma combines both systems into one, giving users the ability to achieve for more than just using one or the other. The impacts to your organization are large –

---

[9]   Oracle White Paper, Lean Performance Management for Public Sector. August 2009

Exceeding Expectations in Any Economy

> "When declining inputs (the real, identifiable causes of the problems) are isolated and improved to optimal levels the output is maximized and the cost is minimized".
> Pete Fisher

increased performance, decreased cost and time, increased consumer satisfaction – both in public and private sectors, and credibility that continues to grow. "Despite the challenges facing government today, it's critical that public sector organizations continue to seek out solutions to improve efficiency, cut costs, and improve their ability to deliver more mission for less cost."[10]

For example, assume a process contains twenty steps and each step takes the same amount of time, with the process taking one hour to complete. The organization addresses the redundancy and waste in the process, and reduces it to ten steps. Now the organization completes the process in half the time, so it is capable of completing two processes in the same time it took to do one before. Essentially the organization has doubled its output in the same time. Attach a cost to the process and it is easy to determine how much time and cost have been saved, all related to the bottom line of the organization's budget.

---

10   Wince, Ron, Lean and Six Sigma in Government: Delivering More Mission With Lower Costs,Guidon Performance Solutions, 2011.

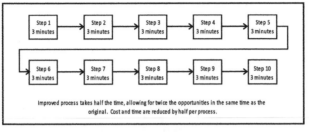

Process map before improvement

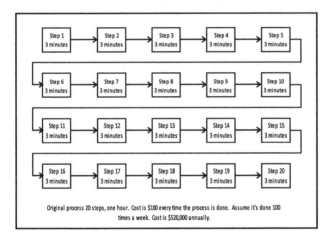

Process map after improvement

In short, Lean equals speed – how fast a process or system moves. By removing any step or process that takes too long or is too complicated, the time to complete a process is shortened. By taking less time, there is less cost, and an ability to produce more services in the same original time. The requirement for success is that processes must be viewed honestly and thoroughly. By doing so the organization creates a culture of continuous improvement, a culture of process excellence.

Sheriff John Rutherford of Jacksonville, Florida, uses the Lean concepts as an integral part of his department. While speaking as the Sheriff, his philosophies and the Continuous Improvement Division are directly applicable to any public or private sector organization. His department, due to Lean, has reduced their budget by more than $30 million, at the same time enhancing the quality and quantity of performance. He talks about creating an organizational climate where people want to achieve, and not perform in an avoidance capacity. He has three core beliefs:

1. "Give them a job worth doing.

   a. They have to see the value in what you're asking them to do – that gets harder the further away from the core mission.

2. You have to remove as many obstacles as you can to them being able to do a good job.

   b. This is where Lean comes in.

3. Reward the behavior you're looking for.

By doing these three things your organization creates a climate where people want to achieve." He talks about organizations that implement all kinds of new processes and hang on to the old ones. The Sheriff's statements directly relate to any organization and provide an operation based on continuous improvement.

Sheriff Rutherford provides examples of how this works in his department. As a case in point he describes a paperwork copying process where his department makes 89,000 copies a week, most of which are discarded or never used. His people did a Lean project and were able to eliminate more than 3.15 million copies annually, a savings of some 25 man years. They were so successful they had to renegotiate their contract with Xerox.

In order to properly apply the Lean Six Sigma methodology, users need to fundamentally understand the following laws. They will guide organizations through the system and its results will prove easier to attain.

1. Law of Complexity: the complexity of the service adds more non-value, cost, and work. The higher the complexity, the higher the cost, the less the value.
2. Law of Focus: 20% of the activities in a process or system result in 80% of the problems. Focus on the 20%.
3. Law of Flexibility: the ability of the process or system to change and become more efficient.
4. Law of Velocity: the higher the number of unfinished tasks, the lower the speed of the process. The

more non-value steps in a process, the slower it is and the more it costs.

Users of Lean Six Sigma have learned the need to identify, reduce, and eliminate suboptimal processes and services by removing activities that provide no value to the organization or its customers. When applying the methodology it gives users a systematic approach to solving their problems. It gives constituents and/or customers more confidence in the systems.

"When I first heard about Lean Six Sigma, I wondered what Lean added to Six Sigma. I found that the answer is speed. The first principle of Lean Six Sigma is: Delight your customers with speed and quality. The second principle says: Improve process flow and speed. Lean Six Sigma emphasizes that speed is directly tied to excellence."[11]

"If Lean Six Sigma has anything to teach us, it is that we should be looking for opportunities to streamline our core processes. It means that we first determine what our core processes are, and then focus on making them flow smoothly."[12]

Experience tells organizations that the right business strategy helps executives and managers create the

---

[11] Poppendiek, Mary, Why the Lean in Lean Six Sigma, page 1, 2004
[12] Ibid

foundation for an efficient and effective organization. The combination of Lean tools and Six Sigma methodologies provides the approach for service organizations that best utilizes the available resources.

Lean Six Sigma

"Six Sigma's goal is growth, not just cost cutting. Its aim is more effectiveness, not just efficiency."[13] Many organizations use Six Sigma for operational improvement, improving existing processes to reduce costs, improve their performance, and provide higher value. Six Sigma is about consistency in a process or system.

Lean originated with the Toyota Production System, developed in the 1920's and 1930's, but actually implemented in the 1950's. The principles were adopted from the U.S. supermarket system, where small amounts of a large variety of products are replaced as customers buy them. Tools that focus on process speed by eliminating waste and inefficiency.

Any activities in the process that do not add value are waste and should be eliminated. It is anything that slows down a process. Fix problems in the shortest time possible with faster execution. The goal of Lean Six Sigma is to establish an organization that operates as effectively as any world class company.

---

13   Byrne, George, Lubowe, Dave, and Blitz, Amy, Driving Operational Innovation Using Lean Six Sigma, page 4, 2007

Exceeding Expectations in Any Economy

With budgets in an ever tightening mode, organizations are under increasing pressure to cut costs. The typical way to reducing spend is to cut services. For example, the City of Spokane, Washington recently told the public they would no longer investigate property crimes – 92% of its workload. Decisions such as this rarely take into consideration the effects on their constituents. Other departments no longer respond to traffic collisions, commercial or home burglar alarms, and a myriad of services previously provided. What is most noteworthy in these times is that departments do continue to send police officers to large numbers of calls that are not aligned with the true mission of the police.

Private sector organizations may react to the need to reduce costs through reductions in force (RIF), cutting services, outsourcing to lower costs in foreign countries, or raising prices in last resort circumstances. The last thing a private sector organization wants to do is raise prices, so the previous alternatives are prioritized. What neither plan for in many circumstances is the longer term forecasting for future years.

The search is on to find ways to cut costs while maintaining the level of service historically provided. Executives and managers normally look at traditional ways in which to achieve these cost reductions. When a new idea is developed, it typically fails, because along the way is becomes easier not to do something hard rather than continue to try and succeed. Decrease your chances of introducing errors in a process. Do tasks faster and cheaper. Remove barriers, obstacles, redundancy from any process and there will be significant reductions in time and cost to the organization

In looking at whether Lean Six Sigma is worth the organization investing in it, look at whose using it now. More than fifty percent of the Fortune 500 corporations use Six Sigma or Lean Six Sigma as part or all of their management of the organization. Those using the methodologies over the past decade or so have reduced their internal costs and increased their profit margin by more than $427 billion. The United States military, the Department of Homeland Security, and other government agencies are using Lean Six Sigma and recognize the value.

Lean Six Sigma serves nine core ideals, articulated in a paper prepared by Jay Arthur, entitled Lean Simplified: The Economies of Speed.

1. "Determine value – what does the consumer want?
2. Use the "pull" system – avoid overproducing and inventories.
3. One-piece flow – make the work "flow", so that there are no interruptions and no wasted time or materials.
4. Level out the work load.

Exceeding Expectations in Any Economy

5. Stop and fix problems to get quality right the first time.

6. Standardize in order to support continuous improvement.

7. Use visual controls so no problems remain hidden.

8. Use reliable technology to support people.

9. Compete against perfection not competitors."[14]

By following these core ideals any Lean Six Sigma undertaking will provide positive results.

For example, the US Army uses Lean Six Sigma as one of its main tools to increase efficiency and reduce cost. In fiscal year 2010, the Army generated $1 billion in cost savings and $3.3 billion in cost avoidance using Lean Six Sigma. In continuing to apply these principles, they make the Army more effective and more efficient.

The US Navy, another example of success, uses Lean Six Sigma across multiple programs. One example was a great need to get Mine Resistant vehicles to combat zones faster. By applying Lean Six Sigma, the demand for 50 vehicles a day was increased to 75 per day. Lean Six Sigma is also used by the U.S. Marines, Air Force, Coast Guard, and the U.S. Surgeon General's Offices. The Department of Homeland Security has also been

---

[14] Arthur, Jay, Lean Simplified: The Economies of Speed.Lifestar 2005

using Lean Six Sigma for several years, with multiple successes documented.

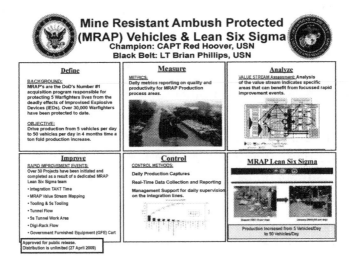

At the local government level, one of the original leaders in the use of Lean Six Sigma was the City of Fort Wayne, Indiana, under the direction of its Mayor, Graham Richard. In his tenure as Mayor he reduced the city budget by some $14 million, with no tax increases. Hartford, Connecticut used it to reduce the processing time for sending checks from their office. Lane County, Oregon has used the methodology in its OSHA regulation process.

Erie County, New York applies Lean Six Sigma at such a rate they created a position for Director of Lean Six Sigma, overseeing projects across all the county's departments. $.15 million saved in 2008, $1.4 million in 2009 and $1 million in 2010 are the benefits so far. The

Exceeding Expectations in Any Economy

City of Morrow, Georgia trained all its department heads in Lean Six Sigma and continues to realize significant benefits. Jacksonville, Florida Sheriff John Rutherford has shaved more than $30 million from his budget using Lean methods.

There are a number of other local jurisdictions that are using Lean Six Sigma – the point being that in the public sector both local and federal governments recognize the value. Just imagine freeing up significant time of your staff and resources. What if you freed up 30% or more of their time? What would you do with it? In essence you are adding 30% more staff at no additional cost. What initiatives, projects, ideas could come to fruition that you didn't do before because you "never had the resources"?

DMAIC

The key to success is focusing on the real problems that are hindering the progress of the organization. It's simply removing the process steps that are slowing it down. By creating excellence and consistency in all processes allows employees to deliver superior results all the time – continuous improvement.

Lean Six Sigma tools can be applied to any organization, regardless of size or type. Processes can be streamlined in any organization. Start with the premise that there isn't a single process that cannot be improved and the organization is on its way. Actually implementing improvement gives employees quick wins and builds their confidence in their ability to bring success to what they do. "Give them a job worth doing."

"Work that adds no value in your customer's eyes typically comprises 50% of total service costs. Improving quality and reducing complexity improves speed."[15] This not an uncommon issue in public and private sector organizations – just ask employees and in some cases, customers, and the answers will provide something of a current status report. Imagine what 50% of your work is costing if it has little or no value.

All work with Lean Six Sigma is tied to the organization's finances – assuring the importance of the work to the success of the organization. All work needs to emphasize system consistency and stability in identifying issues and errors in order to prevent them from happening in the future.

Equally important is to understand what the capability of the processes or systems actually is. It can be alarming to managers to look at the reality of what an organization thinks is working versus what it's actually accomplishing. And when all the numerous processes that are used daily are looked at through an honest lens, the cost in time and money – against the bottom line – are extremely

---

[15] George, Michael L., Lean Six Sigma for Service Outline, page 1, McGraw-Hill, NY, 2003

high. By making relatively simple changes to the way business is done provides significant relief to the burden of diminishing revenue.

For example, assume the organization uses four different processes in its operation. These processes are part of a larger operation in the organization. Looking at each individual part, these processes look like they're performing at an acceptable level at face value. Decisions are made, resources applied, and the end result doesn't look like what was expected.

Maybe it's not exactly where the organization wanted it, but it's doing ok. Then we do a Process Capability assessment and determine that it actually is not what was expected. Now, managers or executives can make adjustments to get the system where it needs to be. And, in applying the Lean Six Sigma tools, the real identification of where changes need to made is now available. Think about the time and cost savings.

Process 1 operates at 97% capability

Process 2 operates at 94% capability

Process 3 operates at 95% capability

Process 4 operates at 93% capability

Now look at the overall capability of the entire set of processes to determine what the impact on the organization is.

Process 1	Process 2	Process 3	Process 4
97%	94%	95%	93%

.97   X   .94   X   .95   X   .93   =

80% yield

meaning that this organization has only an 80% chance of completing these four processes to achieve its goal, without an error. The key is to provide the consumer with a quality service at low cost, when it's needed. Problems with any one of these elements causes problems in the others. There are direct links between these three elements.

The Lean Six Sigma Methodology – DMAIC

- Define: what is the problem to be fixed? validate there is a problem and identify those characteristics that are critical to the quality of the organization. The costs in these cases are unacceptable.
- Measure: what's the current status; where is the problem and to what extent does it exist?
- Analyze: find the real root cause(s)
- Improve: how will the problem be fixed?
- Control: make sure the problem doesn't come back

$Y = f(x)$

Exceeding Expectations in Any Economy

Recalling this mathematical equation from your high school Algebra class, when applied to Lean Six Sigma it is translated into:

The output (Y) is a function of the inputs (x). Looking at the equation as a process or system allows the user to view management of an organization in a simpler, yet far more efficient and effective way. By understanding what goes into a process (inputs or x's), recognition of what the output of the process is (the Y) becomes much easier. For example, look at this graphic, which describes the process in a way that anyone in the organization is able to understand – and affect in outcomes:

$$Y = f(x)$$

$$Y = f(\underbrace{xxxxxxxxxxxxxxxxxxxxxxxx})$$

Result

Inputs

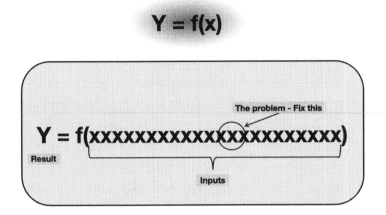

Managers of organizations, when there is a concern or problem typically look at the Y, the output, for causes, an erroneous approach. It isn't the result that needs investigation, it's what caused the problem in the result that does. Lean Six Sigma allows an organization to get there. Considerable personnel hours and resources are spent looking in the wrong places. By following the methodologies in Lean Six Sigma a great deal of time, effort, and cost are avoided or eliminated. This, in turn, allows an organization to take that time and those resources and redeploy them to mission-related activities.

Lean Six Sigma Tools

The following Lean Six Sigma tools are useful in conducting analysis at any level. They provide users with a fast, easy way to produce graphic aids to clearly show prioritization or causation, where the problem is and where resources need to be applied.

- Process mapping – the process map gives the user a graphical representation of all the steps in a particular process. This is one of the best and simplest tools to use. The process map provides the ability to identify what steps in the process provide value and what steps don't. By extracting non-value parts, immediate improvements are made in cost and time savings. The time to complete these graphics is usually small, and the benefits large. By using this tool alone, an organization can realize large-scale benefits over relatively small time periods. The value to the organization is easily recognizable and timed saved alone translates into redeployment of resources.

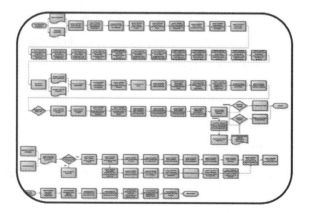

Process map before (as-is)

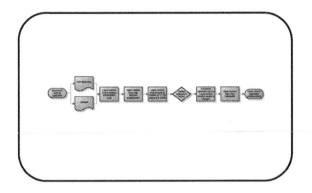

After improvement (should be)

This particular example was completed in about two hours, an approximate investment of about $100. The improvements saved the organization some $165,000 annually; the value proposition in this case alone was that for every dollar that was spent, the organization saved $165.

- Pareto Charts – charts named after Vilfredo Pareto, an economist who determined that 80% of the world's wealth was owned by 20% of the population; the birth of the "80 – 20 Rule". In an organization, the majority of the problems are caused by a few people, processes, or systems. It identifies major causes/categories of problems; they're charted in rank order, providing users with a quick way to determine where to start. The chart orders categories based on volume in each category, showing which category is a priority, and which follow.

Exceeding Expectations in Any Economy

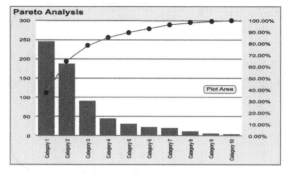

Pareto Chart

- 5 Whys – this simple and time saving method avoids the deeper mathematical analytics and is used to get past the symptom(s) of a problem and move to root (real) causes. By taking a problem and asking why 5 times successively, the user gets deeper into it and ultimately gets to the real cause (or close to it). It's important the user stays honest in answering each why.

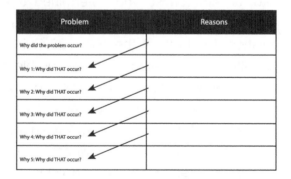

- Run charts – these charts show trends over time, providing the user with a fast way to understand the performance of a process or system. In the example provided, the service level agreement (SLA) was to have these tickets completed and properly closed within 48 hours. The green line represents the SLA, and when the data is plotted in a run chart it is very easy to see that the SLA is not being met in the majority of cases. This leads to asking why and expecting a proper resolution so the problem does not continue, nor does it continue to consume precious resources and time.

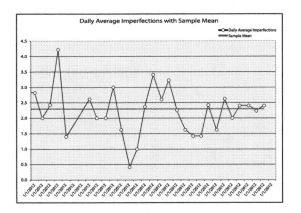

Example Run Chart Over Time

The example below shows an actual application of run charts to demonstrate the success of two initiatives that correlate directly with one another. In this Fortune 200 corporation, employees by the hundreds were leaving their laptop computers unsecured after hours. In addition, tailgating into company buildings was occurring

Exceeding Expectations in Any Economy

frequently – people without an access control card were following employees in, or employees were holding the door to let them in out of courtesy. An assessment showed 56% of people were tailgating in, and Security had no idea who they were. Risk and vulnerability were high, with potential loss of assets and intellectual property at a high level. In essence, the company was easy to access, and once inside the intruder only needed to hide and wait until closing.

Based on the analyzed data, a strategy was developed to reduced tailgating and partner with employees to secure computers. Data continued to be collected and charted to show progress against the strategy. As seen in the run charts here, success was achieved.

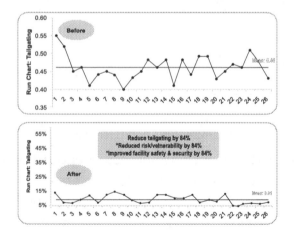

Run Charts for Tailgating

Tailgating was reduced from 56% to 9% in a six month period. Six months later it was at 3%.

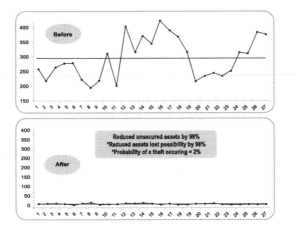

Unsecured Laptop Computers

Unsecured laptop computers were reduced by 98% almost immediately and on average over one year have averaged 98%. The run charts show the progress and graphically represent the wins accomplished in this case. Charts and graphs are able to tell a better story visually rather than the executives reading a text report.

By preparing a set of dashboards representing the information required to make decisions, deploy resources and staff, or allocate other resources give the manager the ability to make faster and more reasoned business decisions. Time and cost are saved again.

Exceeding Expectations in Any Economy

In the case shown here, a service level agreement was established due to service work orders for repairs not being completed in a timely manner in nearly every case. An agreement was reached on a reasonable time to complete and orders were tracked individually. As seen here immediately following the introduction of the agreement, work orders came in on time in nearly all cases. In the cases where the time was not met, managers are easily able to identify exactly which work orders did not meet the agreement and find out why. More savings in time and cost.

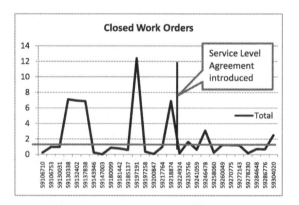

Run Chart showing work order improvement

When corrections are made and re-charted, it is easy to see what the results are. The trend has been in the right direction – proving that the trend shows effectiveness of the strategy.

- Control charts – this tool is used after an improvement is made. The user determines (or the stats program determines), based on the data, what the upper and lower control limits are for a given process. These tell the user whether the corrections made in a process are staying in control or not, and are displayed graphically to quickly see if the system or process has gotten beyond the correction.

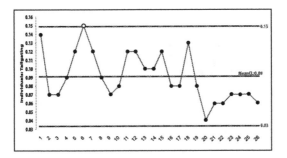

Example Control Chart

- Failure Modes Effect Analysis (FMEA) – this tool provides the user with the ability to prioritize defects/problems based on the level of severity they bring, the frequency with which they occur, and how easy – or not – they are to detect. Each element is given a numeric score on a scale of 1 – 10, with 10 being most problematic. These numbers are multiplied by each other and a Risk Priority Number is calculated. When completed, the higher the number, the bigger the problem, and these problems are addresses in that ranking order.

Exceeding Expectations in Any Economy

Item or Process Step	Potential Failure Mode	Potential Effect(s) of Failure	S E V	Potential Causes	O C C	Current Controls	D E T	R P N
								0
								0
								0
								0
								0
								0
								0
								0
								0
								0
								0
								0
								0

Item or Process Step	Potential Failure Mode	Potential Effect(s) of Failure	S E V	Potential Causes	O C C	Current Controls	D E T	R P N
Apply for and receive permit	City reviews/grants permit	Grant a permit where not appropriate	9	Inadequate review, no sanctions	10	None	8	720
Alcohol served	Overservice of alcohol	Increase risk of problems	9	No checking of patrons	9	Police, Liquor Board understaffed	6	486
Bar overcrowding	Many patrons in small areas	Overcrowding causes problems	9	No Fire Marshal	9	None	9	729
Bar overservice	No checking of consumption	Overservice causes problems	9	No checking	9	None	9	729
Overcrowding outside bars	Too many patrons in confined spaces	Interaction of too many patrons causes problems	7	Crowding inside backs lines up outside	8	Some controls in place by Security	6	336
Disturbances and fights	Small establishments with many patrons	Problems inside cause problems outside	9	Small bars bringing in large crowds	7	None	6	378

Failure Modes Effect Analysis Form

FMEA Completed

In the above example, each step of the process is entered in the far left column. The next column lists what the potential failure could be, and the adjacent column describes the effect of the failure. In the severity column a numeric score is given, followed by the potential cause. Frequency of occurrence is numerically scored, followed by any controls in place. The detection column is scored numerically and the severity, occurrence and detectability columns are multiplied to arrive at a ranking priority number. Those steps with the highest numbers are considered for being the root cause(s).

- Ishikawa diagram (Fishbone) – also known as a cause and effect diagram, allows the user to identify all potential root causes. The problem is identified and placed at the head of the diagram. Potential causes are categorized, typically in the areas of Man, Method, Machine, Material, or Environment any or all of which contribute to the issue. These categories are placed on the "spine" of the fishbone, and causes for each are applied to the specific categories. When completed, the diagram appears to look like a fishbone.

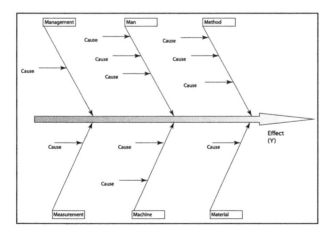

Ishikawa (Fishbone) Diagram

Exceeding Expectations in Any Economy

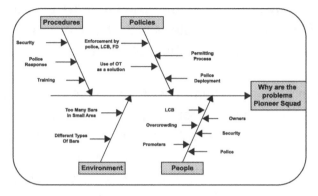

Ishikawa completed

By using any of these tools, and there are others, the organization gets rapid resolution to many of its issues and concerns. Rather than managers speculating or estimating, fact-based decisions are made easier and faster.

Chapter 4:

Lean Six Sigma Case Study:

Bar Problems in an Urban City

"If you want to succeed, you should strike out on new paths rather than travel the worn paths of accepted success." John D. Rockefeller

The target city is in a major urban area with more than 3 million residents in the area. The police department has 1,200 commissioned officers and enjoys a good reputation, but has experienced a few incidents that have created some significant headaches for the department. Among those have been a series of violent incidents in an older part of the downtown area. In about a 5-square block area there are 27 bars.

Several locations have several bars within a 1-2 block area. There are bars located right next to each other, most of different cultures. In front of these bars are vendor food stands. As will be seen, the proximity of these locations to one another and the differences in style of entertainment and culture, result in large crowds gathering within the establishments and also outside waiting to get in. There are some attempts to control access into the bars through security and the formation of lines through rope "fencing". Crowding, traffic problems, lack of emergency access are all collateral issues for the police assigned to the area. Crime in varied forms is prevalent. There are three distinct patrol beats in the area.

Exceeding Expectations in Any Economy

Several different culture bars in close proximity

Traffic due to the bars

As a matter of routine there are usually six officers assigned to the area in three two-man cars. They are supplemented by officers working off duty on overtime in each bar, and special emphasis details associated with the bars – an additional four officers on Friday and Saturday nights. The police department is expending considerable funds to attempt to control the problem.

Another collateral and potentially associated issue is that crime elsewhere in the area is increasing while officers are dealing with bar problems.

In addition to the bar related problems there is frequent and ongoing narcotics dealing, often visible and certainly not unknown as a problem. There are also large numbers of homeless people in the immediate vicinity. While not contributing to the bar problem, their presence in conjunction to the housing, health care, and food services for them, exacerbates crowding and other problems in and around the bars. Special events, such as sporting contests in nearby stadiums, also contribute to crowding, alcohol consumption, and disturbances.

Lean Six Sigma

Lean Six Sigma is a process improvement system, developed by the Toyota Company. A majority of the Fortune 500 corporations have adopted the system, resulting in significant improvements to their operations. Lean Six Sigma is rare in public organizations, such as law enforcement. The Lean Six Sigma methodology follows a well-defined and standardized set of processes and tools (DMAIC). This study has utilized the Lean Six Sigma methodology and tools to reduce the problem to its root causes, identify solutions, and once improvements are made, control and sustain them. The problems created by the bars are the result of systems, both internally and externally. It is the purpose of this study to investigate the defects within the systems causing the problems.

DMAIC

DMAIC (Define, Measure, Analyze, Improve, Control) is a systematic approach to identifying root causes and developing, implementing, and controlling solutions.

Define – validate there is a problem and identify those characteristics that are critical to the quality of the organization. The costs in these cases are unacceptable.

The current police deployment strategy is not working. Though officers have off duty overtime jobs and special emphasis units are assigned the incidents are not being reduced and the problemsremain unresolved.

The officers do a commendable job of reacting appropriately when incidents occur, but the larger question is why the problems occur in the first place. The real problems associated with the bars is overcrowding inside and outside, the proximity of different style and culture bars immediately adjacent to one another, over service of alcohol with few, if any controls, and a significant lack of enforcement. There is little, if any, presence by the State Liquor Control Board, and almost non-existent is the presence of the Fire Department to mitigate the overcrowding problem, the near complete blockage of sidewalks by vendors and crowds, and what would be the complete inability of the fire department to react to a fire in any sort of a timely fashion. The department is essentially the one factor in any attempts to mitigate the problem.

So, ultimately, what is actually causing all these problems? What can be identified as root causes that may be attacked and solved?

To begin to define the problem, it is necessary to visualize the process leading up to the problem. To that end a Process Map is built (Attachment 1).

MEASURE

Over the six week period investigated there were 112 documented incidents in some 20+ bars in the target area. Officers describe the number of incidents as consistent for an approximate eight month period, from March through October. The remainder of the months, November through February, has approximately 75% the activity levels. There are exceptions to the remaining months, typically during holiday periods when activity escalates significantly. In order to remain conservative, the estimate will stay at 75%. For the eight month period there will be an estimated 597 reported incidents. For the remaining four months there will be approximately 238 more incidents, for a total of some 835 incidents in the same 20+ bars, an average of 42 incidents per bar.

As seen in the attachments, charting the data shows this is an unfair characterization of the reality of the data; there are some bars which are overrepresented in activity and others that are underrepresented – the charts actually show where and when the problems are occurring, as well as what they are and how many resources they are consuming. Each event requires about 157 minutes of officer time (2.6 hours) – the annual total of police personnel hours is estimated at 2,223 hours, or an estimated cost of some $104,000 in personnel time alone.

To continue with the Lean Six Sigma approach, the SIPOC tool is utilized – Suppliers, Inputs, Processes, Outputs, Customers – Attachment 2. One element of the tool will provide the process steps necessary to analyze the outputs (problems). Data was collected by a reporting form designed to capture the information related to the bars– Attachment 3. Baseline performance is based on current response and outcomes. In an average year there will be some 835 incidents involving the bars. The cost of responding to these events is ~$104,000, but does not include costs of fire department response, ambulance response, overtime for officers to attend court, costs of court proceedings, medical costs for patrons and police officers, insurance costs, lost wages, backfilling shifts for injured officers, damaged and/or used equipment, property damage.

Bar Problems in an Urban City

Cost of Poor Quality (bar problems) is likely to reach seven figures annually. As opposed to the cost of $55 for a permit, the cost of the bar problems far exceeds the cost of a bar, promoter, or vendor getting a permit. In fact, for every dollar the bar owner spends (permit fee) to the city, the city was spending some $18,181. Hardly a good return for the taxpayer money invested.

ANALYZE

The analysis of the problem identifies the root causes of the problems, validates the causes and identifies the failures and effects. As seen by the charts in the attachment, the locations having the greatest problems, the greatest impact, the greatest consumption of time by officers, and clearly the greatest expense are shown here. In analyzing the problem a series of charts are constructed based on data rather than opinions or guesswork. As already stated, the obvious problems are visible; these, however, are symptoms of real causes.

An Ishikawa Diagram is included to show the relationships and involvement of the various elements leading to the necessity for police involvement (Attachment 4).

The number of events per police patrol shift (Attachments 5 – 6) and day of week is not surprising, with weekend nights being the most frequent (Attachments 7 - 8) as shown in the Pareto Chart and Report. The Pareto Chart (Attachment 9) shows that Bar 1 has the most activity, with the Pareto Report (Attachment 10) showing that nearly one in four calls for all bars are at Bar 1. Bar 2 is second with 9% of all calls, Bar 3 with 8% of all calls and so forth.

Types of police calls are charted,based on department reporting codes (Attachments 11-12). Disturbances, assaults, and assaults with arrests lead the types of calls. The types of calls generated at the bars are based on the most frequent types of calls. Bar 1 stands out, followed by the Bar 2, Bar 3, and Bar 4 (Attachment 13). Bar 1,Bar 3, and the Bar 2 are the spikes in the chart representing the bars requiring the largest number of police officers to respond to incidents (Attachment 14). It is necessary to determine the amount of time officers spend per bar, as well as the amount of time officers spend by incident.

The largest number of officers is spending the most of amount of time dealing with disturbances, assaults, and arrests for assaults. The most time at particular bars officers spend is at Bar 1, Bar 2, and Bar 3 consume the most time by individual bar (Attachment 15).

The larger percentage of time spent dealing with incidents at bars, the larger percentage of time involved in handling incidents, the larger percentage of incidents themselves, the largest number of officers required to handle incidents at bars involve Bar 1, Bar 2, and Bar

Bar Problems in an Urban City

3. Bar 1 is clearly the most troublesome bar. The type of incident most frequently encountered at the bars is disturbances, assaults, and assaults where an arrest is made.

In six weeks there were 112 documented incidents at the bars, or in the near proximity of the bars in this area (including the Bar 2, which is located south of the area). The 112 incidents took 17,386 minutes (290 personnel hours). The incidents involved 533 officers (not individual – this is the total number of officers who responded to incidents; many are the same officer responding to multiple incidents). Fifteen percent of the officers were supervisors. Twenty-nine officers were on overtime or special emphasis patrols dealing specifically with bar issues. As mentioned, this will result in some 2,223 police personnel hours dealing with bar problems – essentially 93 24-hour days (or more than one quarter of a year).

Another issue involved in dealing with the bar problems that is consistent and problematic is the fact that virtually any incident requiring a police response has a large crowd on hand, often hostile and intoxicated, and occasionally assaultive towards the officers. In 17% of the incidents officers were assaulted and/or injured. Crowds vary in size from 50 – 1200 people (Attachments 17 – 21). The total number of officers required to respond to and/or mitigate bar problems is visible in Attachment 22 – as may be seen disturbances, assaults, and assaults with arrests made continue to be the biggest problems. The same incidents also consume the greatest amount of police time (Attachment 23).

As mentioned, given the decrease in activity over the course of the Fall and Winter months, there will occur an estimated 835 incidents with these bar for the year. The cost of conducting police operations in the manner discussed cannot be sustained over time.

A Histogram is provided to show the pattern of time spent, by blocks of time, on bar issues, with the median (average time) time per bar. In the study, the average amount of time per bar incident is 156.63 minutes (2.6 hours) (Attachment 12).

The analysis involves the use of tools to reduce the number of potential causes or symptoms to the critical few that have the greatest impact. The Micro Process Map takes the process steps identified in the SIPOC (Macro Process Map) and breaks out the elements of each. Those elements are transferred to the Input and Y tool (Y represents outputs in the equation $Y=f(x)$ or the output is a function of its inputs), where they are ranked through mathematics built into the spreadsheet. Only those with the highest scoring are moved forward to the Failure Modes and Effect Analysis Chart as we begin to focus towards the critical few causes. These factors are again scored based on their severity, frequency of occurrence, and detectability – also based on formulae built into the spreadsheet. They scored them, resulting in those few factors causing the greatest problems.

In this case, the critical few are identified as the permitting process, overcrowding inside and outside the bars, over service of alcohol. Each of these, or a combination of these, result in the problems police are required to deal with.

IMPROVE

Solutions are based on real causes. Solutions in this case are fairly easy to work, however they require involvement of organizations other than the Police Department.

The specific solutions include

- A permitting process that has enforcement or sanctions capability tied to the location and incidents themselves (as well as eliminating the café seating and outdoor vendors on the sidewalks in the immediate vicinity of the bars).
- The permit requires the owner/promoter to assume the cost and other liability for incidents that occur due to their actions (provable, of course).
- Eliminate hand stamping of patrons that allow them to move freely from one bar to another.

- Involve the Fire Department Fire Marshals in the capacity issue. Progressive enforcement steps would be the rule.
- Help from the Liquor Control Board to work the problem bars would result in sufficient enforcement to reduce the problems.
- Focused and specific actions by the police department, all based on facts and data rather than a "shotgun" style deployment.

Add the elements together and a legitimate goal of 50% - 75% reduction in the target area bar problems within a one quarter time frame is predictable, presuming these solutions occur. Costs are significantly reduced and resources may be focused on other priority police matters. Of note is that police delays and/or lack of consistent response to other crime in the area are noticed by business owners.

CONTROL

To sustain the improvements requires the continual collection of data and a scheduled analysis of the data to identify changes in activity. This assessment needs to be done on a scheduled basis – monthly, quarterly, biannually, depending on the project itself. Any increases in activity at the bars (or in other projects) is identified easily and can be addressed quickly and effectively using facts as opposed to opinion or guesswork. A control plan would include improving the data currently collected.

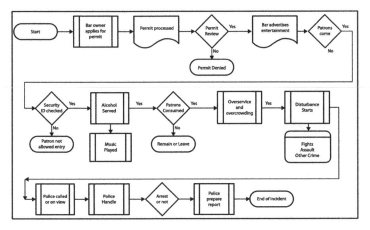

Attachment 1 – Process Map Beginning to End

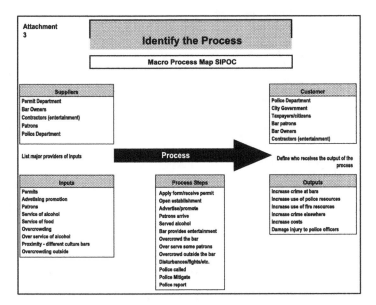

Attachment 2 - SIPOC

Exceeding Expectations in Any Economy

Check applicable boxes and provide selected details:

POLICE RESPONSE

☐ On-Viewed by Officers

☐ 911 calls received regarding event

☐ # of responding officers _____ and supervisors _____

Total time for Primary Unit _____ ☐ check if Mutlti-Officer unit (#) _____ MIR _____

Time for secondary units ____   ____   ____   ____   ____   ____   ____

☐ Officer Assaulted / Injured

☐ Off-Duty ____ or OT Emphasis ____ Unit

DISTURBANCE INFO

☐ # of participants   _____

☐ Crowd size   _____

    Demeanor   _____

☐ Liquor Violations (list on Page 1)

LOCATION INFO

☐ Radio station promotion   _____

☐ Private promoter   _____

☐ Occurred within _____ feet of Mobile Vendor

☐ Additional Ears / Businesses Involved

    ☐ Aristocrats - 220 4th Av. S
    ☐ Bohemian - 111 Yesler Wy
    ☐ Catwalk - 172 S. Washington St.
    ☐ Central - 207 1st Av S
    ☐ Contour - 807 1st Av S
    ☐ Cowgirls - 421 1st Av S
    ☐ Doc Maynards - 610 1st Av S
    ☐ Fado - 8011 1st Av
    ☐ Fenix - 109 S. Washington St.
    ☐ J&M - 2011 1st Av S
    ☐ King Street Bar - 164 S. King St
    ☐ Larry's - 209 1st Av S
    ☐ Last Supper Club - 124 S. Washington St
    ☐ McCoy's - 173 S. Washington St
    ☐ Mediterranean Mix - 205 1st Av S
    ☐ Merchants - 109 Yesler Wy
    ☐ New Orleans - 114 1st Av S
    ☐ Occidental Park - 117 S. Washington St
    ☐ Old Timer's - 620 1st Av
    ☐ Premier - 1700 1st Av S
    ☐ Tiki Bobs - 166 S. King St
    ☐ United Parking - 202 Occidental Av S
    ☐ U-Park - 122 Occidental Av S
    ☐ Wazobia - 170 S. Washington St
    ☐ Other - _____
    ☐ Other - _____

       Place copies of report in "West CPT" and "Community Prosecutor" boxes.

Attachment 3 - Data Collection Sheet

Bar Problems in an Urban City

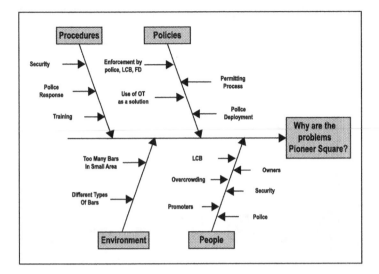

Attachment 4 - Ishikawa Diagram – Potential Causes

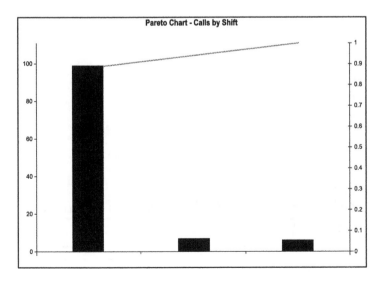

Attachment 5 - Pareto Chart – # of bar calls by shift

Exceeding Expectations in Any Economy

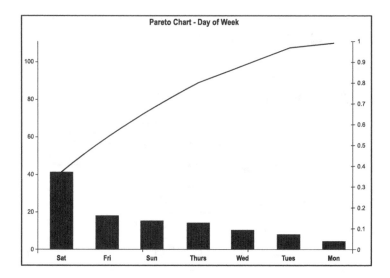

Attachment 6 - Pareto Chart - # of bar calls by day of week

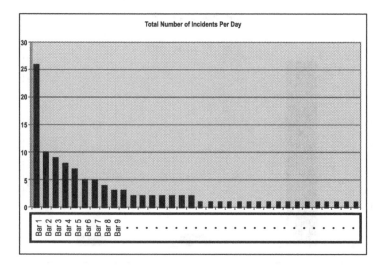

Attachment 7 - Pareto Chart - # of calls by bar

Bar Problems in an Urban City

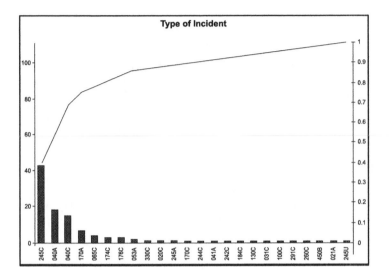

Attachment 8 - Pareto Chart – type of incidents by bar

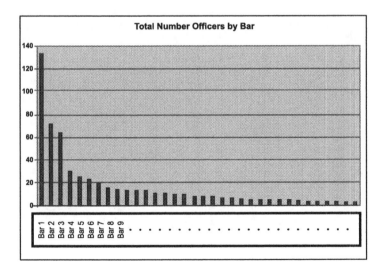

Attachment 9 - Pareto Chart - # of officers deployed by bar

Exceeding Expectations in Any Economy

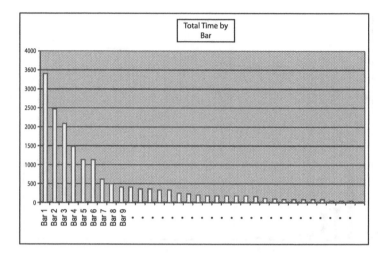

Attachment 10 - Pareto Chart – total time spent per bar

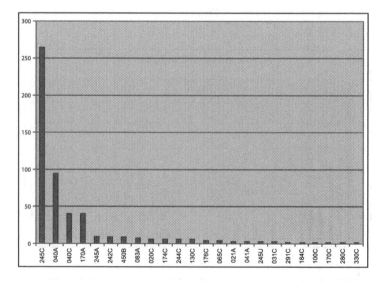

Attachment 11 - Pareto Chart – total officers by incident

Bar Problems in an Urban City

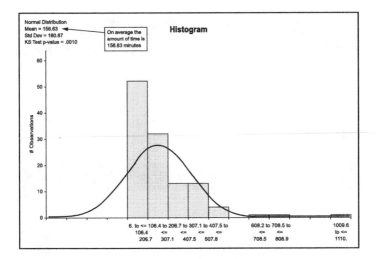

Attachment 12 - Histogram – avg time per call 157 minutes

MicroProcess:						
Step Name	**Description/Details**	**Step #**	**Inputs**	**Controllable Y. N**	**Outputs**	
1. Apply for/receive permit	Bar owners applies for and receives permit from the city	1	Owner applies for permit	N	Owner prepares application	
		1	City reviews and grants permit	Y	Permits reviewed - approved or denied	
2. Open the establishment	Bar owners opens the bar for business	2	Owner prepares the bar	N	Owner receives inventory	
		2	Owner opens the bar to patrons	N	Owner opens the bar	
3. Advertise/promote	Owners advertise entertainment	3	Owner advertises entertainment in various media sources	N	Patrons are advised of entertainment	
4. Patrons arrive	Numerous patrons arrive at bars	4	Patrons go to various bars depending on interests	N	Numerous patrons show up to bars	
		4	Security checks identification	N	Security lines patrons outside; checks ID	
5. Alcohol served	Bars serve alcohol to patrons	5	Hard alcohol, beer served to patrons	N	Consumption of large amounts of alcohol	
		5	Bartenders, employees do not check amounts served individually due to size of crowd	N	Due to large number of patrons, no ability to check over service	
6. Bar provides entertainment	Various entertainment cultures at different bars - proximity to each other	6	Different styles of music depending on bar	N	Different styles, cultures in close proximity	
7. Bar overcrowded	Large crowds patronize bars in close proximity to each other	7	Large numbers of patrons in relatively small establishments	N	Overcrowding	
8. Bar over serves some patrons	Some bars over serve alcohol to patrons	8	Alcohol ordered by large numbers of patrons	N	Over service; intoxicated patrons	
		8	Staffing levels do not allow checking of all patrons for level of consumption	N	Over service; intoxicated patrons	
		9	Bars already overcrowded inside	N	Overcrowding	
9. Overcrowding outside the bar	Bars in close proximity already overcrowded have large number of patrons waiting outside	9	Due to close proximity of each bar, crowds waiting outside for each interact w/each other	N	Overcrowding; intoxicated patrons in close proximity	
10. Disturbances fights, etc.	Overcrowding and over service cause fights, disturbances and other problems	10	Disturbance starts inside or outside	N	Fights, other disturbance	
		10	Overcrowding inside or outside makes situation worse	N	Additional people get involved	
11. Police respond	Police either on-view or are called to incidents	11	Someone calls 911	N	Phone calls to 911	
		11	Police on-view the situation	Y	Police on-view incidents	
12. Police mitigate	Police interdict/resolve incidents	12	Police break up disturbance	Y	Police interdict; injuries, damage may result	
		12	Police make arrests	Y	Arrests if necessary	
13. Police report	Police report the incidents	13	Police prepare reports	Y	Police reports done	

Attachment 13 - Process steps inputs and outputs

Exceeding Expectations in Any Economy

Input & Y Matrix		Number of Bar related incidents	Police Department spend due to incidents	Y	
Rank Importance to Customer		10	9		
Y Description					
CTQ Description		Reduce Numbers of incidents	Reduced Spend	CTQ	Total
Process Step	**Input Description**				
	Owner applies for permit	1	1		19
1. Apply for/receive permit	City reviews and grants permit	9	9		171
	Owner prepares the bar	1	1		19
2. Open the establishment	Owner opens the bar to patrons	1	1		19
3. Advertise/promote	Owner advertises entertainment in various media sources	1	1		19
	Patrons go to various bars depending on interests	1	1		19
4. Patrons arrive	Security checks identification	3	3		57
	Hard alcohol, beer served to patrons	3	3		57
5. Alcohol served	Bartenders, employees do not check amounts served individually due to size of crowd	9	9		171
6. Bar provides entertainment	Different styles of music depending on bar	3	3		57
7. Bar overcrowded	Large numbers of patrons in relatively small establishments	9	9		171
	Alcohol ordered by large numbers of patrons	3	3		57
8. Bar over serves some patrons	Staffing levels do not allow checking of all patrons for level of consumption	9	9		171
	Bars already overcrowded inside	3	3		57
9. Overcrowding outside the bar	Due to close proximity of each bar, crowds waiting outside for each interact w/each other	9	9		171
10. Disturbances fights, etc.					

Attachment 14 - Input and Y Matrix

Bar Problems in an Urban City

Product or Process	Input	Failure Mode	Failure Effects	SEV	OCC	Controls	DET	RPN
1. Apply for / receive permit	City reviews and grants permit	Inadequate review, sanction provisions	Increase police activity and spend; crime	9	10	Few controls issuing permits	8	720
2. Alcohol served	Bartenders, employees do not check amounts served due to size of the crowd	Over service is occuring in the bars	Causing disturbances, fights, crime, increased spend, injuries to patrons and officers	9	9	Police, LCB understaffed in ability to address	6	486
3. Bar overcrowded	Large numbers of patrons in fairly small establishments	Overcrowding and over service cause problems	Increase need for police involvement spend	9	9	Fire Dept needs to be involved	9	729
Bar over serves some patrons	Alcohol provided to persons	Employees unable to check consumption levels	Disturbances, fights, crime increase; increased police involvement and spend	9	9	LCB, Police	9	729
Overcrowding occuring outside bars	Crowding inside backs lines outside, close proximity of bars to each other creates large crowds	Too many patrons in confined spaces	Interaction within crowds causes disturbances; problems inside move outside	7	8	Controls in place by security	6	336
Disturbances, fights, etc.	Large crowds in confined spaces, with alcohol	Small establishments bringing in large crowds	Large crowds in confined spaces, with alcohol	7	8	Few controls in place	9	587

Attachment 15 - Failure Modes Effect Analysis

Chapter 5:

Business Intelligence Decision Support System

"We don't know what we don't know. We can't act on what we don't know. We won't know until we search. We won't search for what we don't question. We don't question what we don't measure. Hence, we just don't know." Dr. Mikel Harry

Business intelligence comes in variety of forms, all of which are useful in their own right. Many are computer based and expensive, others are simpler. The intent is to produce reports useful to management decisions. Business intelligence is information extracted from databases that are able to provide an historic view, current views, and in some cases is predictive in nature.

Its purpose can be to improve the availability and quality of information useful for making more informed management decisions - based on facts. It is very useful in measuring performance and in ongoing improvement programs. The Cooper Model aims to provide users with a simplified, but profoundly successful system allowing users to instantly examine graphic representations of the information, as opposed to viewing numbers on spreadsheets.

This system provides a greater view of an organization's reality, enabling better decisions to be made based on that reality. In this system managers are able to identify areas of poor performance and highlight areas of

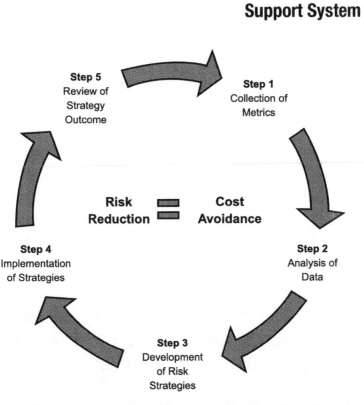

potential future demand/need. Such analytics allow for developing "what-if" scenarios, trends, pattern analysis, and enhanced decision making. Data, properly analyzed, also tells managers whether any changes need to be made and what emerging trends may be identified.

Business Intelligence is premised on defined key performance indicators specific to the organization's expected outcomes, or its mission. "Measurement through Key Performance Indicators (KPI) can provide an important and necessary calibration of performance assuming that alignment exists between the

Exceeding Expectations in Any Economy

organization's mission, structure, supporting processes, and performance tools/measures."[1] Data is compared over time to look for patterns or trends that may affect results. In the case of the Cooper Model, the data is compared week over week, month over month, and year over year.. Its unique approach not only provides the numeric changes over time, but auto populates a series of graphs and charts that clearly show any changes. Gaps are easily identifiable, allowing managers and users to see where something changed, then ask about what happened and what's being done to close the gap.

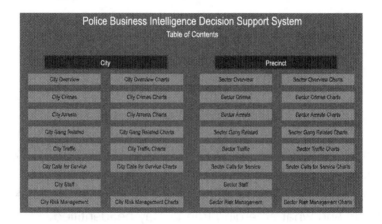

---

1   Oracle White Paper, Lean Performance Management for Public Sector. August 2009

Police Department BIDSS — City Overview

Current Week 2/14/10 to 2/20/10
Previous Week 2/7/10 to 2/13/10
Current Period 1/24/10 to 2/20/10
Previous Period 12/27/09 to 1/23/10

Select Group A Offenses	YTD 2010	YTD 2009	YTD 2008	% Change 10 vs 09	% Change 10 vs 08	2009	2005	% Change 09 vs 05	2009	2000	% Change 09 vs 00
Assault Aggravated	1256	1712	1015	-27%	24%	1712	1545	11%	1712	1342	28%
Homicide	126	121	74	4%	70%	121	100	21%	121	98	23%
Sex Offenses (Forcible)	1944	1694	1648	15%	18%	1694	1234	37%	1694	1254	35%
Robbery	2749	1900	1712	45%	61%	1900	1589	20%	1900	1875	1%
Violent Crimes	6075	5427	4449	12%	37%	5427	4468	21%	5427	4569	19%
Burglary	7117	8227	8224	-13%	0%	8227	6098	35%	8227	6875	20%
Larceny Theft	18242	16700	16841	9%	-1%	16700	15678	7%	16700	13426	24%
Larceny Theft-Theft from Vehicles	7017	6645	5194	6%	28%	6645	6123	9%	6645	5987	11%
Motor Vehicle Theft	1848	1303	1668	42%	-22%	1303	998	31%	1303	1247	4%
Crimes Against Property	34224	32875	31927	4%	3%	32875	26687	14%	32875	27535	19%
Number of Sworn Officers											
Population											
Population per Sworn Officers											

Data collection and analysis

Police Department BIDSS — City Overview

Current Week 2/14/10 to 2/20/10
Previous Week 2/7/10 to 2/13/10
Current Period 1/24/10 to 2/20/10
Previous Period 12/27/09 to 1/23/10

Select Group A Offenses	Current Week	Previous Week	% Change	Current Period	Previous Period	% Change	YTD 2010	YTD 2009	YTD 2008	% Change 10 vs 09	% Change 10 vs 08
Assault Aggravated	28	24	17%	88	88	0%	1256	1712	1015	-27%	24%
Assault Intimidation	32	28	14%	104	104	0%	1323	1454	828	-9%	60%
Assault Simple	136	132	3%	520	585	-11%	7092	6770	6615	5%	7%
Homicide	1	1	0%	6	12	-50%	126	121	74	4%	70%
Kidnapping/Abduction	4	4	0%	14	14	0%	182	78	40	108%	305%
Sex Offenses (Forcible)	48	44	9%	168	168	0%	1944	1694	1648	15%	18%
Sex Offenses (Non-Forcible)	15	12	25%	53	51	4%	718	1820	1840	-61%	-61%
Total Crimes Against Persons	264	245	8%	953	1022	-7%	12631	13848	12060	-9%	5%
Burglary	128	124	3%	488	488	0%	7117	8227	8224	-13%	0%
Counterfeiting/Forgery	12	18	-33%	54	54	0%	688	662	335	1%	98%
Destruction of Property/Vandalism	336	332	1%	1324	1320	0%	17693	20874	16619	-15%	26%
Fraud Offenses	140	140	0%	540	536	1%	7075	6436	6454	10%	0%
Larceny/Theft	344	340	1%	1352	1352	0%	18242	16700	16841	9%	-1%
Larceny/Theft-Theft from Vehicles	148	144	3%	568	568	0%	7017	6645	5194	6%	28%
Motor Vehicle Theft	52	48	8%	184	184	0%	1848	1303	1668	42%	-22%
Robbery	56	52	8%	200	200	0%	2749	1900	1712	45%	11%
Stolen Property Offenses	160	156	3%	616	616	0%	8077	8270	7027	-2%	18%
Total Crimes Against Property	1376	1354	2%	5326	5318	0%	70466	71017	647074	-1%	11%
Drug Equipment/Violations	228	224	2%	888	888	0%	11743	144	112	8055%	29%
Drug Narcotics/Violations	182	188	-3%	734	734	0%	9391	176	144	5236%	22%
Prostitution	56	52	8%	220	220	0%	2646	208	176	1172%	18%
Weapon Law Violations	60	66	-9%	256	256	0%	2900	240	208	1108%	15%
Total Crimes Against Society	526	530	-1%	2098	2098	0%	26680	768	640	3374%	20%
Total Crimes	2166	2129	2%	8377	8438		109787	85434	76774	29%	11%

Data Collection and analysis

Exceeding Expectations in Any Economy

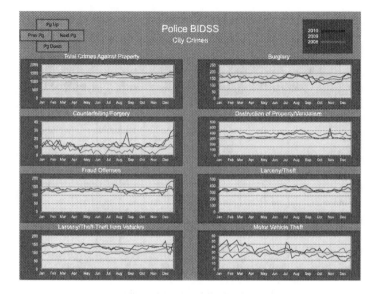

Graphic representation of the data

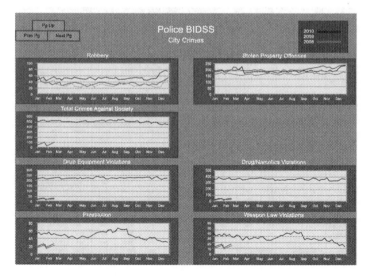

Graphic representation of the data

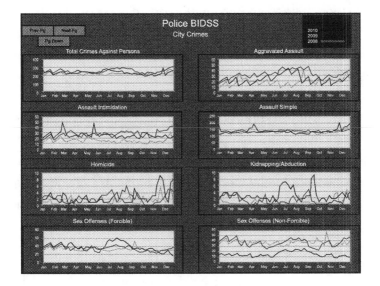

Graphic representation of the data

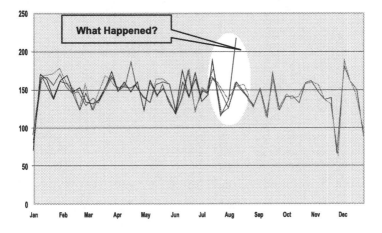

BIDSS chart showing spike analysis

Exceeding Expectations in Any Economy

For the public sector, including cities, counties, law enforcement, and local government, there are immediate and long-term benefits in using BIDSS rather than the CompStat, CitiStat, CountyStat and other similar programs. These programs use spreadsheets containing numeric data compared over time. The Cooper Model refined this into a graphical representation of the information that allows more rapid decision-making, an easier way to view performance against expectations, and reduces the amount of time to do so. It allows the organization to look forward and plan accordingly.

Activities	Current Week	Previous Week	% Change	Current Period	Previous Period	% Change	YTD 2011	YTD 2010	YTD 2009	% Change 11 vs 10	% Change 11 vs 09
Requests for Service	220	292	-25%	1029	1140	-10%	8203	8172	12145	33%	-32%
Tier 1	220	292	-25%	1029	1140	-10%	8201	8123	12123	34%	-32%
Tier 2	0	0		0	0		2	49	14	-96%	-86%
Tier 3	0	0		0	0		0	0	8		-100%
Safety Issues - Total	19	8	111%	47	42	12%	192	228	144	-16%	33%
Personal	0	0		0	1	-100%	2	5	6	-50%	-78%
Fire Related	0	0		0	0		1	8	8	-99%	-83%
Maintenance	7	3	133%	14	10	40%	87	113	129	-23%	-33%
Overheating	12	6	100%	33	31	81%	102	102	0	0%	
Safety Issues - Total	28	38	-26%	124	95	31%	888	771	1665	13%	-53%
Restricted Doors Not Secured	3	2	50%	11	3	267%	123	188	82	-35%	-34%
Computer Not Secured	17	18	-5%	56	38	471%	327	319	696	3%	-53%
Other Devices Not Secured	0	4	-100%	7	0		48	58	592	-21%	-82%
Sensitive Information Not Secured	0	0		0	0		0	1	12	-100%	-100%
Interior Security Doors Not Secured	2	10	-80%	28	29	-3%	235	82	71	155%	231%
Exterior Doors Not Secured	6	3	-100%	21	21	0	122	87	244	40%	-50%
Locks Not Working	0	1	-100%	1	2	-50%	11	15	55	-27%	-80%
Card Readers Not Working	0	0		0	2	-100%	4	11	101	-54%	-86%
Alarms - Total	1	4	-75%	8	4	50%	30	28	3	7%	800%
Fire	0	0		1	1	0%	5	11	0	-55%	
UPS	0	0		0	0		0	0	0		
Crisis Alert	0	0		0	0		5	1	0	400%	
Crisis Alert - False	1	4	-75%	5	3	67%	20	16	0	25%	

A sound business intelligence system provides an organization with a better view of its reality and its reality compared to its universe of business or service. It additionally provides better decisions based on that reality, identifies areas of poor performance, and will highlight areas of current and potential future demand.

Based on the very successful and not infrequently used CompStat system, four questions are asked in any meeting where business analytics are to be presented. These four questions form the foundation of reasoned ability to make decisions grounded in fact rather than speculating. They provide the organization also with accountability that is across all levels of the organization and allows for developing strategies based on fact as well.

1. What's working....why?
2. What's not working....why not?
3. If it's not working what could we or should we do about it?
4. What new strategies need to be developed and implemented?

In terms of these questions it is important that executives and managers receive answers that give the reality of the situation. Those giving the answers need to be precise about what it is they actually did that worked, or not, what it is they actually did to continue succeeding. If the answer is not to that extent, managers or executives need to be asking for specifics. Notes need to be taken of any task or follow-up needing completion and at the immediate following meeting, those who were assigned tasks must be prepared to report on the current status. In short, the organization is managed for results.

Exceeding Expectations in Any Economy

Information transitioned into near real-time intelligence is useful to users in decision making and allocation of finite resources, optimizing what the organization already has rather than a continual ask for more staff and more money that may not be needed in the first place.

CompStat is a powerful, adaptable data analysis tool that helps describe the current level of operational efficiency. It helps identify problem areas and constantly measures changes in conditions. This gives management the real-time information it needs to make timely, critical problem solving decisions. This transforms the problem solving management style from "reactive" to "proactive". It also ensures that implemented solutions are kept on track and that resources are applied in the most expedient, efficient way (minimal waste).

As part of the "continuous improvement process", CompStat is used to constantly measure the results of implemented solutions developed in the Six Sigma Process against two significant benchmarks. These benchmarks are: (1) the original condition (before improvements/solutions were applied); and, (2) the expected/intended outcome. CompStat gives you real time data that tells you how well the solution is working. This real time data allows managers to make adjustments in a timely manner so that resources are focused appropriately - not wasted).

Support System

The first step in any business intelligence system is the collection of data – data that is relevant to the operation and expected outcomes. Once the data is gathered it is necessary to fully describe it. This is descriptive statistics – organizing the data so relevant information can be quickly understood and applied. A second significant use of descriptive statistics is to assist managers and executives understand the relationship between trends, patterns, incidents, or events that provide managers qualification and quantification of the strength of relationship among the data – cause of concerns or predictability of outcomes – does one element have an effect on another, and what does it mean?

The second use of data is comparative statistics, useful for analyzing data to compare trends or patterns, year over year, month over month, or any other similar trend useful to decision making. Such data, transformed into information, and then into actionable business intelligence provide the organization with a structure for successful decisions and management, as well as a culture of accountability.

The key feature of any business intelligence or statistical analysis program is that the data must be accurate and thorough – it must have integrity or it becomes useless. It is also required that such intelligence be shared so a system of consistency is developed.

Exceeding Expectations in Any Economy

The importance of basing a management tool on numerically recorded, empirical data cannot be understated. By definition, empirical data is first hand knowledge recorded by those that experienced or observed an event. It is necessary for the Business Intelligence Decision Support System that such data be recorded in numerical form. Through this process the manager or executive is presented with fact-based data that is well defined and unaffected by the degrees of separation between the event and the manager.

The manager is then able to utilize a whole host of well-established statistical and graphical tools to analyze the numerically formatted data. A benefit of this is that there is no need to develop and validate new processes by which data is analyzed. In addition, should the results of the analysis be challenged they can be well defended from critique by the weight of history showing the analytical methods be to be accurate and sound. Through the analysis of data the manager can determine where problems exist, types of correlation between data groups, and whether any refinement of data is required.

The results of analysis provide the manager and executive with a list of short term goals and the means through which to measure the success of any corrective action. For example, should the analysis suggest that a disproportionate amount of resources are being used to complete a lesser function the immediate plan would be to reduce them to a specific amount or level. Once the plan has been implemented, continuing data analysis provides direct and immediate feedback on the level of success. Where the original analysis placed the amount of resources at a given level, continuing analysis will show if these levels change and by how much, thus providing a percentage of goal completion.

Due to its nature, the Business Intelligence Decision Support System requires participation of all members within the organization being managed, and when used properly, can provide significant positive feedback. It is in the best interests of the managers when devising a plan to talk with those who have gathered the data, and who are most intimately familiar with the situation. The manager can then leverage this to show that the work each member accomplishes is important and directly affects the goals of the organization.

The Business Intelligence Decision Support System is flexible to a manager's changing area of responsibility due to its nature of mathematical analysis. How the data is analyzed, how goals are set and measured, how a manager engages the entire team – Business Intelligence Decision Support assists with these responsibilities that are independent of how the environment may change. The manager focuses on the analytics and their results. This allows the manager to continue to use the Business Intelligence Decision Support System as he/she moves through the levels of management, or between departments or companies.

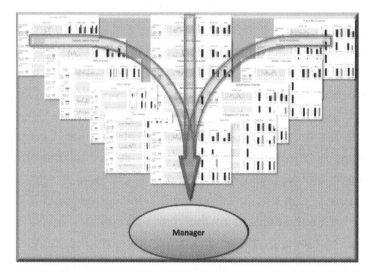

Require every level of the organization to have a clear understanding of:

- Why the organization exists – it fundamental goal
- What the organization values
- Its vision for the future
- The critical performance measures that will make a real difference to your performance
- How you determine resource allocation

Chapter 6:

Employee Involvement

"A successful team is a group of many hands, but of one mind." Bill Bethel

The Mutual of Omaha Company prides itself on what its employees are involved in. "Mutual of Omaha employees have always been committed to lending a helping hand when it is needed most. Whether it's responding to the needs of fellow co-workers, donating resources to victims of tragedies or volunteering countless hours in the community, Mutual's employees are constantly giving back ."

The Weyerhaeuser Company is another company that involves its employees, also in external activities that benefit the community. They state "We invest in our communities because when they grow stronger, we all benefit ."

Pitney Bowes is a successful corporation, and their employee involvement program again speaks to external assistance. "We know that good corporate citizenship helps us to attract and retain good employees. We also know that our people can develop useful skills outside the workplace, and we believe that encouraging engagement in our local communities reinforces the engagement in our company."

Exceeding Expectations in Any Economy

Companies speak frequently and appropriately about employee involvement and the ongoing theme is working with the community to make it a better place to live. In the private sector this is an excellent philosophy with extraordinary results and partnerships. While this enhances the company reputation and its customer base, many organizations do not use their employees as a force multiplier in making the company more efficient and effective in all its systems, processes, and service delivery. By doing so, costs are reduced, time is freed to be used on more mission critical activities, and profit is increased.

For example, from a security point of view, the employees are provided brief training and policy regarding the protection of assets and intellectual property. Such training, unless practiced as a matter of routine, or reminding them regularly, may not provide the level of protection required to maintain the integrity of the corporate assets or people. The cost of loss can be staggering to a company, especially as it relates to intellectual property. If not practiced or reminded, such information will not become a regular part of an employee's daily mindset. As a consequence, the levels of risk and vulnerability escalate. Lax behavior on the part of employees does relate to an increase in policy violations, loss, and damage.

Corporate Security's responsibility is to assure assets and people are protected, that a safe and secure environment is provided for all staff and assets. In reality, Corporate Security tends to follow a law enforcement management and deployment model. Security officers are deployed as access control agents, roving patrol officers, and officers who respond to calls for service – most of which are typically non-urgent incidents. Officers are trained, but not normally to a significant level, and compensation is low. The officers are also normally from a contract security organization and tend not to be full time employees of the company. Corporations use contract security to keep costs down.

The Corporate Security model, as with the police, is historically risk-averse and reactive in nature. The Cooper Model, applied in the private sector, transforms Corporate Security into a proactive, problem identification, intelligence-based deployment model, premised on achieving measurable results. Where the Cooper Model has been deployed, major results in the reduction of risk and vulnerability, reductions in cost, cost avoidance, and performance enhancements are dramatic.

To discuss the success of the model, two Fortune 200 corporations are presented. Results include the reduction in budgeted dollars in one case by more than $900,000 and in the second by more than $750,000. At the same time, the level and quality of performance increased substantially, bringing reductions in risk and vulnerability in the high 90% range – all maintained over a multi-year timeframe. The second case occurred when budgets were being reduced across the board in the corporation.

To apply the Cooper Management Model requires an organization to apply its security management in a slightly different approach. The application of philosophies of performance excellence and optimization of existing resources is required to succeed. Service delivery is premised on using each element of the model in conjunction with the others. High standards and absolute integrity are essential, as is allowing officers the ability to help build and apply the system. By doing so Security becomes part of who they are and what they do. They own making it work and take pride in their accomplishments. By implementing this system the officers begin to engage corporate employees and include them in securing themselves and their assets – again, employees become a force multiplier for Security, a partner that provides an environment that allows the company to have a workplace free from problems and disruption, all helping to enhance the company's EBITDA (earnings before interest, taxes, depreciation, and amortization – in other words, profit).

Corporate Security takes ownership in bringing the model and its call to action in using it. The security management team uses the model as its management philosophy and transitions to a proactive model. Steps include:

1. Training personnel on what the model is and how it works.

2. Applying the model as the management philosophy for Corporate Security.

3. Developing and implementing the Business Intelligence Decision Support System – giving Security a focused approach to the security and safety problems encountered.

4. Introducing and training management team members in Lean Six Sigma. To increase use and effectiveness, apply the Lean Six Sigma Simplified system.

5. Introduce security officers to the employee involvement element of the model. Train officers in proactive methods for patrolling the facilities. Rather than the random patrols they make (which produce random results), officers are required to proactively look for safety and security problems, then escalate them to the people responsible for them. Officers then follow up to assure the problem has been reconciled. Officers in the field are the most closely positioned to such problems and are best positioned to provide solutions – listen to them.

6. Develop a reporting system to assure that results are being achieved.

In visiting a few of the results of the proactive approach, officers discovered the following, the remediated it with the appropriate personnel to assure reconciliation of the problem:

- Discovered hundreds of pages of documents mark as company intellectual property lying on top of shred bins; anyone could have picked it up.

- Hundreds of endorsed checks , some in the tens of thousands of dollars left on desks in the Finance area after hours. Anyone could have taken them. By working with the Finance personnel, the concerns were completely eliminated.

- Access card keys issued to employees or contractors who forgot their badge were left lying around cubicles and offices by the hundreds. These cards could be used by anyone to enter the buildings after hours. Officers worked with managers to describe a working solution and return rate went from 39% to 95%.

- Tailgating into buildings was reduced from 56% to 9% and continuing.

Each of these wins were developed and introduced by security officers at little or no cost. They understand the value of proactive measures; looking for and escalating problems to the right people, then assuring they are followed up on to correction. Staff is far more focused and not random. They fully understand that random patrols produce random results, and focused, proactive patrols produced targeted results aligned with their mission.

To engage corporate employees, Security needs to know what the problems affecting employees are. Asset protection becomes a primary target for Security to quietly and subtlety attack – to lower the possibility of security breaches first, and if a breach occurs, lower the possibility of an asset loss. This asks the question of how easy a breach may occur, and secondly, if one does, how easy is it for the perpetrator to remove assets, including intellectual property or proprietary information.

The typical breach of a secure facility occurs by a perpetrator tailgating into a locked building. A corporate employee, issued a card access badge, uses the badge to swipe the reader, opens the door, and enters. Employees, in efforts to be kind or polite, often allow people they don't know to follow them inside. Perpetrators may capitalize on these kindnesses by walking up carrying items and an employee will hold the door. Others may tell an employee they forgot their access badge, or the weather is an issue. Once inside, the person is able to reach much of the facility and simply wait for an opportunity to take assets.

The first question to ask is whether breaches may be a problem. Data must be collected over time to determine the level of tailgating by counting the number of people entering the facility, and the percent who are tailgating in. Data also needs to be gathered on the level and types of loss the company is experiencing, and correlating loss with breaches – they usually relate. Officers on patrol then gather information on the number of unsecured assets, emphasizing laptop computers and cell phones, as well as other data storage devices.

As an example, in one company, officers found that 56% of the people entering a critical building were tailgating – Security had no idea who these people were or what they were doing. At the same time Security Officers found some four hundred unsecured laptops in the same building. The level of risk of loss and vulnerability to breaches was unacceptable. Security Officers were tasked with finding ways to reduce the numbers to an acceptable level – and did.

Addressing vulnerability of the facilities, officers made themselves visible at key entrances where tailgating was prevalent. Officers asked those entering to display their badges, and to those who didn't have one, officers verified they wereemployees, and reminded the employees about corporate policy regarding the display of badges at all times. In addition, the officers created professional signs reminding all those entering of "One card, one swipe". Over time the number of tailgaters was reduced from 56% to 6%.

In addition to attacking tailgating the officers developed a Security reminder Card, a professionally printed card reminding employees to secure assets. The card contained the date, time, and officer name if any questions arose. On their now proactive patrols, officers looked for unsecured assets and on finding one or more, would leave the Security Reminder Card on the person's desk. Officers were not permitted to touch anything, only place the card on the desk. They also took the name and office number and entered them into a database. Over time, unsecured assets were reduced by 98% and over a three-year period have stayed at or near that level. Repetitive offenders are referred to the Security senior management team for follow-up.

The **SIMPLE TRUTH**
is that **WE FAIL**
to **ASK** ourselves
what we **LEARNED**
AFTER we **LOST**
our **PRECIOUS**
RESOURCES
and **PEOPLE.**

Chapter 7:

Community Involvement

"What do we live for, if not to make life less difficult for each other?"
George Elliott

In the law enforcement world, policing has changed over its life in the United States. From the Political to the Reform Eras, the Professional Era to the introduction of the Community Policing Era in the 1980's, the police have grown to large extent in the way police services are delivered. The introduction of Community Policing was an attempt to reengage the police with their neighborhoods, business, and educational institutions – to form real partnerships to solve community concerns and problems.

Community Policing was designed to move the police from a highly mobile, yet detached service model back to a system that forced interaction with the residents and business owners. Departments had to rebuild vision and mission statements, as well as their deployment models to meet the new requirements. To meet the needs for new officers to populate new programs, the federal government introduced grants to allow departments to fund positions and varied programs they otherwise would be unable to afford. Thousands of police officers were hired, training in Community Policing provided, programs implemented, and partnership requirements described.

Officers were assigned to foot patrols, bicycle patrols, schools (School Resource Officers, DARE officers, Gang Officers), or could be assigned to Neighborhood Police Stations. All these had in mind to create more visibility and partnering with the community, at the same time identifying local problems and creating solutions for them. The goals were reduction of crime and the enhancement of the quality of life for residents and business.

Since inception, Community Policing has largely failed to transform quality of life issues and crime reductions. The addition of enhanced 911 services actually exacerbated the problems departments are facing. Calls for service continue to climb, and there are fewer officers to respond. As a consequence, the police are now cutting core services. Budget requests for more officers are failing due to reduced revenue in the local jurisdictions and due to competing priorities. Departments are continually being asked to do more with less, and it's likely the trend will continue.

A number of departments were asked to estimate the percent of calls being made to 911 lines that were actually related to emergencies. Estimates were consistent – between 80% and 90% of calls coming in on 911 lines were not emergencies, and a large percent of those are calls that have no business being made to the police. Such calls include:

- Questions about pet licensing

- Bus schedules
- How to pay a bill
- Time of day
- Voting information
- Trash removal schedules
- Young children not getting out of bed to go to school
- Sprinklers touching the neighboring lawn
- Not enough pizza sauce on the pizza
- Service at the restaurant wasn't fast enough

The list goes on and on – any department can provide its own list of such calls. The critical question, because departments will send officers to these calls, is what is it costing? Have the police "evolved" to the point of want a cop, get a cop? We should be assuring people that real action is being taken to enhance their security and safety and quality of life.

What percent of your department's calls for service or other activities are in line with the reason you exist? What amount of time do they consume? What is the effect on your ability to actually reduce crime? What is it costing? More critical, what can you do about it?

Now, compare that against the response of the police to actual criminal acts – the real reason the police exist.

Departments, in many cases, will no longer respond to crimes. The police, in many cases, do not respond to home or commercial burglar alarms, they do not respond to most traffic collisions, they do not respond to property crimes – nor investigate them, but they will send officers to calls such as those listed previously. Why? What is the cost?

Chief Joel Schults of Adams State College in Colorado wrote an enlightening article for the International Association of Chiefs of Police. In the article he asked, "What did community policing teach us "? he states that if community policing isn't already dead, let's kill it and move on. The Chief said that he "liked solving problems and working with the public ." He further states that some success was achieved, such as a change in thinking and that the police did engage with the community, to an extent. His most cogent argument is as follows, "When we do collaborate, we need to narrow our focus to those objectives that are likely to produce results that are in line with our purpose. We must distill the purpose of policing down to its essentials and stop trying to be all things to all people under the guise of doing community policing ."

The Chief is right. What the police have actually accomplished is to continue to add to their already growing burdens. No effort was ever made to engage the people in policing themselves – as taught by the experts, the police. What has been accomplished is to teach the public that whatever their issue or problem is, all they need to do is call 911 and someone else will handle it for them. This model simply is unsustainable.

Is there a better, smarter way to manage what the police do? The issue is further complicated with the case closure rates in the United States. Property crime cases are closed at rates in the teens. Violent crime cases are closed at rates in the mid-40% range. In essence, about two-thirds of the people who are victims of crime do not get their cases closed. Yet, the police are hiring the most intelligent, educated police officers in history and do have the best technology ever.

There is a better, smarter, and easier way to address Community Involvement and associated crime and quality of life issues in any community, and the cost of implementation is minor and involves time only. The return on the investment in that time is phenomenally high. The police can expect to:

- Reduce crime by double digits
- Reduce calls for service by twenty to thirty percent or more
- Free the time associated with these calls to redeploy existing resources to the community's priorities
- Identify significant cost avoidance associated with these calls – stabilize the departmental budget

- Create real, long-term partnerships with the community
- Enhance the credibility of the police department, internally and externally
- Increased problem solving capability for the department
- Greater support or the department
- Less strain on finance and personnel

In addition, by applying the model, citizens and the local government get a better view and understanding of the capabilities, the mission, and the limitations the police face and an increased awareness of the issues and challenges facing the department.

To accomplish this is relatively easy, but the department must commit to the time necessary to implement this model. To do so, follow these steps:

1. Identify all the neighborhoods in the city or county (or precinct); they need to be relatively small (on the order of no more than 20 – 30 homes).
2. Rank order these neighborhoods by the number of police calls for service; regardless of the type of call.
3. Set up a neighborhood meeting; most or all of the homeowners need to be present. Work the meeting time to their best schedule.

4. Identify the purpose of the meeting; its main idea is community preparedness – what neighbors need to do to help one another in a major disaster. Advise them that in such an event police, fire, medical will very likely not be available to them for a considerable period of time, and that they need to help one another.

5. At the meeting, have each person identify himself/herself and what they do. Are there medically trained people, people with special skills or equipment, vehicles, or who are able to assist the elderly?

6. Once the neighbors are comfortable in the setting, a police administrator should be present to show residents the numbers and types of calls the police have responded to in their neighborhood for the past five years. Attendees should be provided a list of these calls, most of which they'll see are unrelated to why the police exist.

7. The administrator should discuss the impact of these calls on finite police resources and the ability of the police to react to crime or other quality of life issues due to their involvement in these unrelated calls. The discussion should also include the time and cost associated with these non-mission calls.

8. The administrator should pointedly ask all the neighbors and residents to help the department by not calling 911 before acting locally to mitigate the

> minor neighborhood concerns; by doing so, the resources freed up for the department to focus on crime or other quality of life concerns.
>
> 9. The police should ask for some level of commitment from the people in helping the department – most people will help if asked.

Once the first neighborhood is done, go to the next on the list, then the next, until all neighborhoods have been met. The police department needs to understand that not all people will be willing to engage, but most will. Not all police calls will be handled by the public, but any percentage is a success.

As an example, assume the department handles 100,000 calls for service annually. Assume that 50% of calls are non-mission and that each call takes an average of one hour to complete. This equates to 50,000 calls officers are responding to that should be handled by the community, or 50,000 personnel hours being used unnecessarily. Assume also that each officer makes $50 per hour in salary and benefits. This is the equivalent of about 25 police officers being wasted, at a cost of $2,500,000.

Now, having all 50,000 calls handled by the public is both unrealistic and is not achievable. Taking the example one step further, assume that half of the 50,000 are handled by the public; 25,000 calls. Here is the equivalent of twelve police officers at a cost of $1,250,000 being wasted. This is time and money better used on mission-oriented activities such as crime, drugs, gangs, traffic, or whatever the department priority is. Assume it's 10%, or 10,000 calls. This equates to 5 police officers at a cost of $500,000. Any decrease in these types of calls is a large win for the police.

Peripheral benefits include lower crime, lower numbers of calls, the ability to focus resources where they're needed, lower cost and cost avoidance, true partnership with the community, enhanced credibility with employees, the local government, and the community. These wins represent the real purpose of community involvement – get the community involved in policing itself and enhancing its quality of life – all while working with the police and not expecting more from them than they are capable of delivering. Imagine accomplishing all this when the economy is down and revenues are decreasing.

Chapter 8:

Predictive Analytics

"Every great achievement was once considered impossible." Unknown

The use of predictive analytics in both the public and private sectors is increasing. In the public sector they are useful in law enforcement as a legitimate statistical probability of any future event occurring based on historic information in a set of criminal events, for example.

Spatial Analysis and Mapping

The idea behind analyzing the times, dates and locations of activity is not new. In fact, many organizations use "Forecasting" when dealing with various incidents and activities. For example, this forecasting model simply uses means and standard deviations to calculate the probability an incident will occur between specific dates, times, days of the week and within certain geographical areas. The following section will provide more details about the specific calculations used.

As an example for a police agency, one urban department was suffering a series of armed robberies of fast food restaurants. To properly complete this analysis there needs to be at least three events, ideally in the same geographic area, by the same suspect(s). The department provided information about three such cases in a smaller geographic area. This information included the dates, times and locations of the incidents.

The time and day of week probability was calculated by identifying the most frequent occurrences and then graphing the information. This analysis is necessary because it shows trends. Looking at the department information, it is apparent that the instigators prefer to rob locations at night and not on days that are typically busy.

To calculate the probable date range for the next robbery, it is necessary to know the spread of the data. Specifically, this requires counting the days between incidents and then taking the mean and standard deviation. The mean provides the average and the standard deviation the distribution of the days between each incident. This data is then used to predict the next robbery event.

One standard deviation above and below the mean will result in a 68% probability the next robbery will occur between the two dates. Assuming a normal distribution, 68% of the data will fall within one standard deviation. Then moving outward, there is a 95% probability a robbery will occur within two standard deviations and a 99% probability within three standard deviations of the mean. When examining the higher probabilities, the user finds greater time and geographic spread, making the 68% probability the best estimate for action.

The spatial analysis of the incidents requires a mapping program and to geo-code the incident location. Then just like calculating the date range, the mean and standard deviation of the latitude and longitude coordinates are calculated. Next, to find the distribution of the locations, calculate the distance between each site and the mean. Then the standard deviation is taken to find the distribution of the locations. Starting at the mean, there is a 68% probability an incident will occur within one standard deviation, 95% probability within two standard deviations and 99% probability between three standard deviations.

The goal of this model is to identify probable dates, times and areas so that resources can be adjusted accordingly. These calculations will allow the organization to provide appropriate support to high risk areas.

The spatial analysis model, as seen, is useful for predicting criminal events, such as robberies, burglaries, thefts, and any other crime with three or more occurrence as described. In the private sector the model is useful for similar internal incidents, again depending on the ability of the data to meet the criteria of the model. Local government may find it useful for mapping and predicting a variety of incidents, such as traffic problems for Public Works or Engineering.

Example of arson cases:

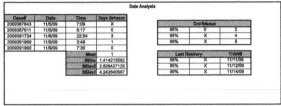

Date Analysis

Case #	Date	Time	Days Between
2009387843	11/5/09	7:09	X
2009387811	11/5/09	6:17	0
2009391734	11/8/09	22:54	3
2009391869	11/9/09	3:49	1
2009391960	11/9/09	7:30	0
		Mean	1
		StDev1	1.414213562
		StDev2	2.828427125
		StDev3	4.242640687

Confidence		
68%	0	2
95%	X	4
99%	X	5

Last Robbery		11/9/09
68%	X	11/11/09
95%	X	11/12/09
99%	X	11/14/09

Day of Week Analysis

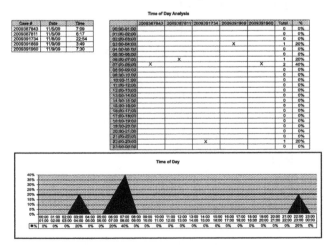

	%	Count
Monday	40%	2
Tuesday	0%	0
Wednesday	0%	0
Thursday	40%	2
Friday	0%	0
Saturday	0%	0
Sunday	20%	1

Day of Week

	Monday	Tuesday	Wednesday	Thursday	Friday	Saturday	Sunday
■%	40%	0%	0%	40%	0%	0%	20%

Day of Week

Initial data analysis

Time of Day Analysis

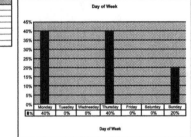

Case #	Date	Time
2009387843	11/5/09	7:09
2009387811	11/5/09	6:17
2009391734	11/8/09	22:54
2009391869	11/9/09	3:49
2009391960	11/9/09	7:30

	2009387843	2009387811	2009391734	2009391869	2009391960	Total	%
00:00-01:00						0	0%
01:00-02:00						0	0%
02:00-03:00						0	0%
03:00-04:00				X		1	20%
04:00-05:00						0	0%
05:00-06:00						0	0%
06:00-07:00		X				1	20%
07:00-08:00	X				X	2	40%
08:00-09:00						0	0%
09:00-10:00						0	0%
10:00-11:00						0	0%
11:00-12:00						0	0%
12:00-13:00						0	0%
13:00-14:00						0	0%
14:00-15:00						0	0%
15:00-16:00						0	0%
16:00-17:00						0	0%
17:00-18:00						0	0%
18:00-19:00						0	0%
19:00-20:00						0	0%
20:00-21:00						0	0%
21:00-22:00						0	0%
22:00-23:00			X			1	20%
23:00-00:00						0	0%

Time of Day

	00:00 01:00	01:00 02:00	02:00 03:00	03:00 04:00	04:00 05:00	05:00 06:00	06:00 07:00	07:00 08:00	08:00 09:00	09:00 10:00	10:00 11:00	11:00 12:00	12:00 13:00	13:00 14:00	14:00 15:00	15:00 16:00	16:00 17:00	17:00 18:00	18:00 19:00	19:00 20:00	20:00 21:00	21:00 22:00	22:00 23:00	23:00 00:00
■%	0%	0%	0%	20%	0%	0%	20%	40%	0%	0%	0%	0%	0%	0%	0%	0%	0%	0%	0%	0%	0%	0%	20%	0%

Time of day analysis

Exceeding Expectations in Any Economy

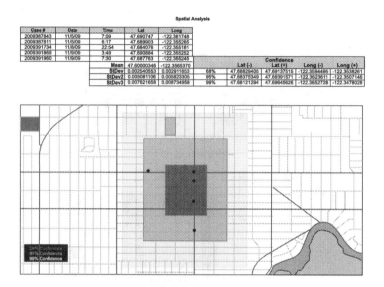

Spatial Analysis

Case #	Date	Time	Lat	Long		Confidence			
2009387843	11/5/09	7:09	47.690747	-122.361748					
2009387811	11/5/09	6:17	47.689903	-122.355265					
2009391734	11/8/09	22:54	47.684076	-122.355181					
2009391869	11/9/09	3:48	47.690884	-122.355252					
2009391960	11/9/09	7:30	47.687763	-122.355245					
	Mean	47.60000346	-122.3565370			Lat (-)	Lat (+)	Long (-)	Long (+)
	StDev	0.002540553	0.002911653	68%		47.68829405	47.69137515	-122.3594495	-122.3538261
	StDev2	0.005081106	0.005823305	95%		47.68375349	47.69391571	-122.3623611	-122.3507145
	StDev3	0.007621658	0.008734958	99%		47.68121294	47.69645626	-122.3652728	-122.3478028

Spatial analysis

Earned Value Management

Earned Value Management was created in the 1960's as "a project management system that combines schedule performance and cost performance to answer the question, 'What did we get for the money we spent?[1] It takes the basic concept of measuring budget to actual and adds the question of what the project got for the money it spent.

The Cooper Management Model took the Earned Value model and modified the concept to address workplace violence as a predictive tool. Having achieved success

[1] Successfully Presenting Earned Value, Your Guide to Earned Value Management, 2005 KIDASA Software, Inc.

in that realm, the model can be applied to any number of public and private sector activities, such as budgeting, performance management, and other opportunities.

In the workplace violence world, the Earned Value concept was organized to compare the actual number of cases against the projected number. The third element was modified to what the level of severity of each case was, then look at severity versus number of case to form the ability to project workplace violence over time. Given this intelligence, organizations are able to create and implement mitigation or preemption strategy. This also is measured in the Earned Value model.

As may be seen in the example below, an actual application of the model, the lower line represents the projected number of cases for the year (based on historic data). The middle line represents the actual number of cases, so managers can see immediately that the actual number is greater than projected, and the variance is growing. The top line shows level of severity; in this case it is measured on a scale of 1 – 4, with decimal-place increments.

Exceeding Expectations in Any Economy

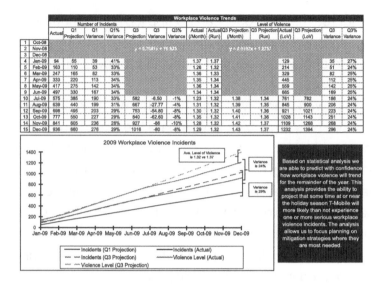

In looking at the chart on a monthly basis, it is easy to see that not only is the number of cases higher than expected, but the level of severity is increasing as well. Mid-year, the organization is able to project the remainder of the year (dotted lines), and initiate mitigation strategies. Mid-year the organization estimates it will have at least one and probably more serious workplace violence cases by the holiday season. By following the solid lines, some of the strategies worked as the number of cases and level of severity decreased from projected expectations.

The following year, the previous outcomes were used to project workplace violence for the year. The successes and strategies from the previous year were enhanced and applied and the increase in success is obvious – although still not where the organization needs it to be.

	Number of Incidents								Level of Violence			
	Actual	Q1 Projection	Q1 Variance	Q1% Variance	Average (/Month)	Average (Run)	Q1Projection (Month)	Q1Projection (Run)	Actual	Q1 Projection	Variance	Variance %
Jan-10	99	78	15	16%	1.37	1.37	1.37	1.37	127	107	54	27%
Feb-10	162	156	6	4%	1.23	1.30	1.37	1.37	290	214	49	25%
Mar-10	252	234	18	7%	1.24	1.28	1.37	1.37	123	321	71	22%
Apr-10	140	112	19	5%	1.15	1.30	1.37	1.37	428	427	98	28%
May-10	417	190	27	1%	1.22	1.28	1.37	1.37	656	164	121	22%
Jun-10	500	468	22	1%	1.23	1.27	1.37	1.37	687	548	117	21%
Jul-10	688	540	25	4%	1.50	1.28	1.37	1.37	227	748	158	22%
Aug-10	845	824	21	1%	1.52	1.28	1.37	1.37	533	855	182	22%
Sep-10	712	703	10	1%	1.19	1.27	1.17	1.17	106	952	184	21%
Oct-10	768	780	-12	-1%	1.12	1.28	1.17	1.17	581	1069	213	22%
Nov-10	112	858	-26	-1%	1.27	1.28	1.17	1.17	1062	1176	230	22%
Dec-10	936	906	-14	-1%	1.37	1.28	1.17	1.17	1189	1140	265	22%

2010 Workplace Violence Incidents

Incidents (Q1 Projection) Incidents (Actual)
Incidents (Q3 Projection) Violence Level (Actual)

For this example a third year was developed and part-way into the year the lessons learned have allowed the organization to reduce the number of cases and reduce its risk and liability, as well as its costs and time.

2011 Workplace Violence Trends (Q1 Projection Based on 2009 & 2010 Total)												
	Number of Incidents								Level of Violence			
	Actual	Q1 Projection	Q1 Variance	Q1% Variance	Average (/Month)	Average (Run)	Q1 Projection	Q1 Projection	Actual	Q1 Projection	Variance	Variance %
Jan-11	71	78	-7	-10%	1.30	1.30	1.30	1.30	92	101	21	23%
Feb-11	165	156	9	5%	1.26	1.28	1.30	1.30	211	203	46	22%
Mar-11	247	234	13	5%	1.38	1.31	1.30	1.30	324	304	77	24%
Apr-11	322	312	10	3%	1.17	1.28	1.30	1.30	412	406	90	22%
May-11	390	390	0	0%	1.21	1.26	1.30	1.30	493	507	103	21%
Jun-11	455	468	-13	-3%	1.37	1.28	1.30	1.30	583	608	128	22%
Jul-11	522	546	-24	-5%	1.31	1.29	1.30	1.30	671	710	149	22%
Aug-11	595	624	-29	-5%	1.23	1.28	1.30	1.30	781	811	166	22%
Sep-11	669	702	-33	-5%	1.30	1.28	1.30	1.30	867	913	188	22%
Oct-11	728	780	-52	-7%	1.27	1.28	1.30	1.30	932	1014	204	22%
Nov-11	201	858	-57	-7%	1.25	1.28	1.30	1.30	1023	1115	222	22%
Dec-11		936								1217		

2011 Workplace Violence Incidents

Incidents (Q1 Projection) Incidents (Actual)
Incidents (Q3 Projection) Violence Level (Actual)

Exceeding Expectations in Any Economy

Another example is provided, useful for both the public and private sectors, involves managing the organizational budget. By applying the methods and principles, managers can forecast whether they will be over, under, or on budget for the year. It allows for mid-course corrections as necessary or appropriate.

In this case the budget line items are provided, as well as actual as they are obtained. The model calculates the projected outcome for the month and graphs the budget to actual and projected numbers. By viewing the report monthly, weekly, or as often as the manager chooses, the budget can be successfully managed.

Department	Actual	Projected		EVM
$187,207.50	$214,756.50	$214,756.50	$0.00 $	187,207.50
$187,207.50	$401,964.00	$401,964.00	$187,207.50 $	374,415.00
$187,207.50	$589,171.50	$589,171.50	$187,207.50 $	516,622.50
$187,207.50	$776,379.00	$776,379.00	$187,207.50 $	748,830.00
$187,207.50	$963,586.50	$963,586.50	$187,207.50 $	936,037.50
$187,207.50	$1,150,794.00	$1,150,794.00	$187,207.50 $	1,123,245.00
$187,207.50	$1,338,001.50	$1,338,001.50	$187,207.50 $	1,310,452.50
$187,207.50	$1,525,209.00	$1,498,465.07	$160,463.57 $	1497,660.00
$187,207.50	$1,712,416.50	$1,658,928.64	$183,386.94 $	1,684,867.50
$187,207.50	$1,899,624.00	$1,819,392.21	$182,841.14 $	1,872,075.00
$187,207.50	$2,086,831.50	$1,979,855.79	$182,217.38 $	2,059,282.50
$187,207.50	$2,274,039.00	$2,140,319.36	$181,504.50 $	2,246,490.00
$2,246,490.00				$ $2,246,490.00
		Difference	-$106,170.64	

Year	$ 2,246,490.00	
Month	$ 187,207.50	
Day	$ 6,154.77	

Budget spreadsheet with calculations

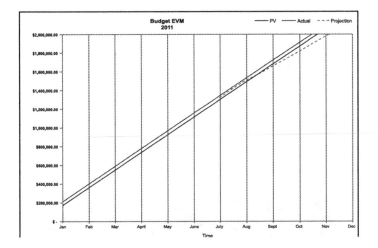

Earned Value model

In this example, the organization will end the year slightly under budget.

The value of this model is significant:

- Measures performance against expectations and allows for forecasting performance;
- Provides an early warning system, allowing organizations to address issues and make reasoned mid-course corrections;
- Demonstrates the effectiveness of those corrections;
- Variances allow forecasting and progress is measurable

EMBRACE

systems thinking

which **cultivates**

process excellence.

Chapter 9:

Local Government

"The golden rule for every businessman is this: put yourself in your customer's place." Orison Marden

The use of business principles in local government has been around for more than a decade. The specific use of Lean Six Sigma has been part of various municipal governments, including Fort Wayne, Indiana, Buffalo, New York, Eric County, New York, Hattiesburg, Mississippi, and Jacksonville, Florida, to name a few. They understood the premise that government has waste and redundancy, they set about to make their localities more aware of how to eliminate those problems and maximize the use of the tax dollars collected, and the employees who work there. They learned quickly to look at their jobs differently, and that when waste is eliminated, their work becomes quicker and more efficient.

The local government, the city or county council or the mayor or county executive, are responsible for managing the jurisdiction's priorities, goals, and objectives. They disperse the tax revenues to the departments to accomplish the overall mission of the city or county. They must make often difficult decisions, frequently following legitimate arguments from department heads over whose priorities are more important. All too often the priorities are aligned with public safety being the primary recipient of the dollars over other competing interests. And, as mentioned earlier in the book, public safety produces some of the lowest outcomes of all departments in terms of its mission and purpose. When the economy is down the decisions become all the more difficult and even amount to reductions in staff and service. By applying the Cooper Management Model the local government has a combination of the best business principles that alone would produce measurable results, but combined will provide the local government with outcomes beyond their expectations.

This is done through the various departments and the revenue collected through taxation. In today's economy, the taxpayer is substantially more inclined to demand a more efficient, effective use of those dollars to bring the expected quality of life and key services. They want better service at lower cost, and want more transparency in how it's done. The local government has the responsibility to answer to those demands. A greater use of proven business principles is a growing trend, but considerable work remains to be done – government is still inefficient and ineffective to a great extent.

To accomplish successful key services the local government must drive the departments to a more careful planning and implementation cycle and align the departments more closely to bring those services. The local government becomes responsible for identifying and removing all the barriers to collaboration and accomplishment. They need to provide the direction and guidance in optimizing the resources and staff departments have, and link performance directly to efficiency and effectiveness. The departments need to be trained and the culture shifted to achievement.

Government leaders also need to be keenly aware that revenues will continue to diminish for the foreseeable future and plans must be made to accommodate a growing service demand with fewer resources. Focused decisions, based on analyzed business intelligence, must be made to provide the best outcomes.

Of all the business principles being used by local government, the most common is Lean Six Sigma. They do so largely because Lean Six Sigma is able to produce rapid results, and through a culture of continuous improvement system, results keep occurring. In addition, Lean Six Sigma is easy to use and training is fairly inexpensive. Lean Six Sigma also allows the local government to avoid cutting services, as is traditionally done in a down economy; rather, waste is cut and key services protected, perhaps even enhanced.

By applying the Lean Six Sigma methodology, the local government begins to achieve considerable success and bring levels of service and efficiency to the community they have not experienced before. By applying the other elements of the Cooper Model and with Lean Six Sigma, the local government crafts a strategy and ability to bring levels of service that dramatically optimize dollars and resources. Local government, by its nature, captures considerable data and information.

By using the Business Intelligence Decision Support System – taking that data and information and transforming it into actionable intelligence then further focuses finite resources. They begin to identify and attack root causes of problems rather that symptoms. This enhances decision-making ability and affects outcomes in a substantially positive way. Decisions are based on facts rather than intuition or guesswork, and provide appropriate direction to users in solving problems. The system also acts as a performance accountability system.

The third element of the Cooper Model is Community Involvement. As articulated in the earlier chapter, working in partnership with the community in all elements of quality of life – not just policing – creates an environment conducive to high standards. Community members become a force multiplier for the finite resources the city or county has. Costs are reduced, activities are lowered, strain on resources is reduced, issues are resolved, performance improves, and the credibility of the local government is enhanced substantially.

ESTABLISH your value proposition – your BUSINESS CASE for QUALITY

Chapter 10:

Value Proposition

"Price is what you pay. Value is what you get." Warren Buffet

Definition – it is the unique value the organization brings to its customers or constituents. It is why customers will do business with the organization or why constituents will support an organization. "It is a clear, compelling and credible expression of the experience that a customer will receive from a supplier's measurable value-creating offer".[1]

Value propositions work because they force the organization to focus its resources where they are needed. This is particularly important in difficult economic times because it is essential that resources that are committed have the best chance of success.

Every penny saved goes to the bottom line.
  • Speed up time to make decisions
  • Increased revenues
  • Lower costs
  • Decreased expenses
  • Reduced labor costs
  • Improved efficiency
  • Faster time to completion

---

[1] Kaplan, Robert S. and Norton, David P., Winning Value Propositions, Page 1, 2009

- Streamlined processes
- Maximized productivity
- Faster response times
- Improved asset utilization
- Decreased attrition; reduced costs
- Minimized risk
- Improved customer retention
- Increased competitive differentiation

These points are what executives want and need to hear.

The value proposition of the organization asks the following types of questions. By conducting an honest assessment of the organization, answering these questions puts it in a better position to state its abilities to provide higher quality service at lower cost. The competitive differentiation is obvious.

- Where does your organization excel?
- What does your organization do that helps lower its costs and increase profit?
- What does your organization do that helps improve quality?
- What are the core competencies and capabilities of the organization?
- What does the organization do better than anyone else?

- What benefits does the organization provide to users, better than they could do before?

- What does your organization do to help others achieve their goals and objectives?

- What does your organization do that shows measurable results?

  » Increased service

  » Faster service

  » Decreased costs

  » Improved productivity

  » Increased profit for the private sector organization

Mike Schultz and John Doerr, on the Rainmaker Blog, provide a succinct and genuinely complete description of what a real value proposition needs and do it in 3 steps to craft a "winning value proposition":

1. Potential buyers have to need what you're selling. It has to resonate with them.

2. Potential buyers have to see why you stand out from other available options. You have to differentiate.

3. Potential buyers have to believe that you can deliver on your promises. You have to substantiate."[2]

These three steps apply to both public and private sector organizations. In the public sector, people need the services government provides – police, fire, mail, etc.

---

2   Schultz, Mike and Doerr, John, 3 Rules to Building a Value Proposition That Sells Like Crazy, Rainmaker Blog, 4-15-2010

The difference with the private sector is that the credibility of the organization and service delivery needs to resonate in order to maintain support for those services. In the private sector, the definition is much easier as services and products must be something the consumer wants and it has to be better than the competitor, and promises made must be promises kept – the guarantee. The public sector bases its success on its actions in service delivery, the quality, and competition with other public sector organizations for finite dollars.

In terms of value and a return on the dollars invested, the organization should be asking and answering the following questions:

- If the organizational management system is inadequate or not performing to capability what is the financial impact?
- What are the financial costs associated with less than adequate management?
- What is management doing that is most cost effective?
- Elements of the Value Proposition should include the following when describing what your organization brings:
- Lower costs – save money
- Time savings – doing more in less time – also relates to lower cost

Exceeding Expectations in Any Economy

- Increased productivity – delivering more of the service in less time
- Lowers risk
- Lowers vulnerability
- Increases credibility
- Competitive differentiation – why your organization is better than the competition; the benefits of your organization
- How your organization optimizes its resources to deliver

To be successful the customer or constituent has to believe your organization provides service value superior to any alternative they may consider. It is your organization's responsibility to provide them the difference.

Calculating Value Proposition

The equation: Value Proposition = Benefits - Cost. Defining the benefits the organization provides needs to be done.

- What does the organization value?
- What does the customer value?
- What does the community value?
- What does the local government value?

For the private sector, a strong value proposition to create competitive differentiation, specifically a "unique selling proposition" for their goods or services is essential to their success. It addresses customers and draws them to buy. The private sector value proposition should contain specificity in numbers or percentages to demonstrate proof in the product or service. In applying the Cooper Management model in two corporations, success is demonstrated by stating "With today's economy bringing the struggle to reduce costs, we saved them over $750,000 in just one year." Or, "With today's need to maximize existing resources and staff, we reduced risk of loss of unsecured assets by 98% in just two months."

In the public sector, including local government and city or county departments, the focus is on showing value to their constituents (taxpayers) in the services that are being provided at a very cost effective level. The value to the constituents is that the community is safer and the quality of life issues are minimized. Fewer interruptions that disrupt their ability to lead a normal life is a true value in any community.

For example, in the chapter about creating real partnerships with the community, the police work with the neighborhoods, businesses, and schools to place much of the activity with people who are far better able to address them than the police, who are overburdened. The value proposition is that both are aligned with community quality of life and issues actually get resolution. Such an approach can be stated, "As a result of the police-community partnership, police calls for service are down 23%, and the time freed for the police department resulted in a 7% higher case closure rate." It's about focus, and in order to focus, the obstacles and barriers need to be removed (Lean Six Sigma). All being said, the community is able to realize real value for the dollars it invests in the local government. The credibility of the mayor, council, department heads is significantly better.

As a final example to illustrate the value for the taxpayers, a good tool is the use of a process map. In the private sector, organizations will use technology to secure assets – alarms, card keys for access control, cameras, and other measures. Such technology costs to purchase and install, and costs to maintain. In one of the companies referred to in this book, their command center monitored cameras and digital video recorders remotely. Of the 10,000 cameras and 8.000 recorders, many would fail, be out of focus or blocked, or pointed in the wrong direction.

By moving into a proactive management model, the command center began monthly reviews of all cameras and recorders, identifying which was working properly and which wasn't. Those that weren't generated a work order for immediate repair. This eliminated the risk of incidents or events occurring that were not captured and significantly reduced corporate liability – again, time and cost savings.

To start the proactive model required the command center to know its existing process – the as-is. Then, with a review and extraction of the non-value added steps, the should-be model was adopted. Savings due to the process being re-engineered, on an annualized basis, resulted in a 6-minute per camera review being reduced to 2 minutes per camera. With an average of 50,000 reviews per year, and 3 minutes per camera saved, some 2,500 hours are saved each year. At $30 per hours in salaries and benefits, reduction in cost equals nearly $75,000.

Including the time to create the process maps and make the changes in procedure (one time events), that time was about five hours. Cost to produce is about $150. Value proposition is Benefits minus cost. $75,000 - $150 = $74,850. The Value Proposition statement may then refer to the fact that for every dollar invested, nearly $500 was saved. This, combined with the process maps visually showing the improvements, tells customers or constituents a compelling story.

PROVIDE

SOLUTIONS

to common sense

PROBLEMS

EVERYONE

SHARES.

Chapter 11:

The Value of Your Money

"No one can possibly achieve any real or lasting success by being a conformist." J. Paul Getty

The value of money speaks to whether or not an organization has obtained the maximum benefit from the goods and services it provides. The main question to be asked and answered is whether or not the organization has obtained the maximum benefit from the dollars it receives – in terms of:

- Quality
- Cost
- Resource use
- Fitness for the purpose of the dollars
- Actual value obtained

This book has clearly shown a new and unique management model that provides, regardless of size or service, significant wins in terms of cost and time savings. The Cooper Management Model shows how to optimize resources and staff, even in the face of reductions in revenue. In this economy money is tight and likely will continue to be for the foreseeable future, so executives and managers must adjust their managements system and practices to assure not only survival, but to retain or enhance the quality and quantity of their product or service.

Exceeding Expectations in Any Economy

Customers or constituents are demanding faster service, better quality, all at a lower cost. Those organizations, public and private, who don't adapt to ever changing financial environments will not remain competitive (in the private sector) or will not survive politically or financially (in the public sector). Applying this model creates the opportunities to achieve high level outcomes, and send the message to customers or taxpayers that your organization really values the dollars they are spending on you, and that you are optimizing the resources and staff you already have. This is what they want to hear – that their concerns are valid and are being heard, and action is being taken. They care about this, and the organization is providing them the knowledge, expertise, and solutions necessary to meet economic and other challenges.

They want results – it's that simple, and this model gives it to them. The value of their money is further manifested in the form of higher morale and performance of employees, higher quality and quantity of service, and improved productivity in spite of fewer employees. Risk and liability are lower in some cases, and all these benefits are visible to the organization's constituents.

To provide specific information to them, ask the following questions and make the answers visible to them. Using these questions will vary from private to public organizations.

- "How does your product, service, or solution impact your customer's bottom line or expenses?
  - » What costs have been eliminated?
  - » What time has been saved?
  - » Can you quantify a tangible hard dollar value gain?
- What positive impact has your product, service, or solution had on bringing additional revenue or business to your clients?
  - » What has the gain been?
  - » Can you determine a tangible hard dollar value gain?
- Does your product, service, or solution enable your customer to achieve any competitive advantage?
  - » What has the gain been?
  - » Can you determine a specific hard dollar value gain?
- How has your product, service, or solution impacted your customer's bottom line or expenses?
  - » What costs have been eliminated?
  - » What time has been saved?
  - » Can you quantify a specific hard dollar value gain?" [3]

Once you have articulated the value of their money in your results, the information needs to be evangelized.

3   Konrath, Jill, Developing Strong Value Propositions, 2009

Exceeding Expectations in Any Economy

Develop a set of talking points, or scheduled reports to highlight the results achieved. Put it on the website and marketing materials for the private sector, and on the local government or department website. Put the information in newsletters or as a supplement inside monthly bills – show people the organization is really doing something to give the taxpayers value for their dollars.

Chapter 12:

Tying the Model Together

Any part of the model works well as a stand alonemanagement practice or principle. In fact, each has proven very successful in its own right, and the majority of corporations are using them. A few local governments or departments are using Lean Six Sigma or some form of data or statistics to review performance. The strength of each is amplified significantly when they are combined with each other to form the Cooper Management Model.

Community or employee involvement reduces the burden on an organization by acting as a force multiplier. This is one of the largest positive impacts the organization can realize… the Business Intelligence Decision Support System laser focuses your resources where they are needed, to identifiable, identified problems or concerns. Lean Six Sigma reduces time and cost even further by removing barriers and obstacles from your systems and processes. Predictive analytics, in some cases, may forecast or predict some types of incidents or events with statistical probability.

Put the parts of the model together and…

1. Community or employee involvement reduces the burden on an organization's staffing and resources significantly, freeing time and cost to deploy

where needed. More emphasized focus results in improved quality and quantity of service

2. Lean Six Sigma – eliminates suboptimal processes and systems, further reducing time and cost, making those resources available. In freeing time and cost, that time and cost takes existing resources and staff and redeploys them to true mission-oriented activities.

3. Business Intelligence Decision Support laser focuses those resources to exactly where and when they're needed to what they are needed for. The intelligence gives users the ability to instantly view trends, gaps, or patterns, then deploy to them.

4. Predictive analytics – allows organizations in some cases to forecast events or incidents and develop preemptive strategies using the Business Intelligence system.

As stated, the individual parts of the model have been or are being used with success. However, given the reduced revenue, the expectation of delivering substantially more with substantially less, organizations find themselves struggling to meet those requirements. Many organizations face ongoing reductions in staffing, budgets, and other resources they view as necessary to do the work. There is the value of the Cooper Management Model.

By combining these proven management systems into one comprehensive system, the outcomes increase dramatically. Rather than one element working for the organization, there are up to four and the combination enhances that even further. Each element of the model has a relationship with the others; each works in conjunction with the others to produce a cause and effect relationship, giving customers and constituents more than the value they are expecting. The model also sets any organization's competitive differentiation at a level higher than expected.

"It is **BETTER** to **SOLVE PROBLEMS** than **CRISES.**"

John Guinther

Chapter 13:

Getting Started

As has been discussed throughout this book, the organization must do something to survive in this economic environment. Based on the Cooper Model, the organization achieves more than survival, it enhances its mission and outcomes to a level not previously attained. It's a function of getting started – taking the first step.

By following this advice, the organization is able to fulfill its mission and objectives at a faster speed, with better quality, and at lower cost – in any organization.

1. Understand that what you're doing can be done better;
2. Challenge the status quo – everything can be improved;
3. Focus on achieving goals and objectives;
4. Focus on success – place responsibility for the future squarely on your own shoulders;
5. Understand the reality that it's up to you to decide to move forward;
6. Get clarity in your thinking – clarify goals and objectives; think smarter, not harder;
7. If the organization doesn't like the results it's getting, change methods and thinking;
8. Find new ways of handling old problems;

9. Contribute to the organization at a higher level than before;

10. Be responsible; commit to the highest standards of integrity and ethics;

11. Always have a can-do, positive attitude; tell yourself what you can do, not what you can't.

12. You make a difference in what you do, so act like it does;

13. Don't give up – get and keep a competitive spirit and philosophy;

14. Stop trying to keep everything the way it is – things will never be the same again;

15. Change – your organization needs to change. By not adapting, the organization begins to decline;

16. Stop explaining failure; explain success;

Move forward! Use this model to manage your organization beyond expectations. Most are not operating at peak efficiency, yet year after year continue to ask for more resources and staff. They don't get the resources requested and the typical response is to cut services in the public sector or raise prices in the private sector. This approach, especially in local governments, is used year after year with the same outcomes. Even in today's economy, departments and government follow the same stale and unsuccessful model. Resources and staff continue to be lost, yet few think or act beyond the traditional approach. It becomes irresponsible at some point to continue down this path without investigating every way to improve efficiency and effectiveness.

When an organization does not consider the benefits here, it will continue to deteriorate, lose customers or credibility, and everyone loses. It becomes a simple matter of trying something that does work rather than continuing to use systems that don't. Applying the Cooper Management Model is not difficult or time consuming. It is not a long journey and each step taken produces good, positive results.

Any organization can improve its outcomes by using the Cooper Management Model.

Imagine the possibilities!

"The **FUTURE DEPENDS** on **WHAT WE DO** in the **PRESENT.**"
Mahatma Gandhi

Let your
FINANCIAL SYSTEM
do what it was
INTENDED TO DO
– give you the
FOUNDATION
for **GOOD BUSINESS**
DECISIONS and **ENABLE**
COORDINATION
of the organization
TOWARD THE GOALS.

171

Exceeding Expectations in Any Economy